Obsessive Compulsive Disorder

D1561049

Obsessive compulsive disorder (OCD) is characterised by a person's obsessive, distressing, intrusive thoughts and their related compulsions. It affects an estimated 1 per cent of teenagers and has been detected in children as young as three years old.

In this concise, accessible book experienced contributors provide detailed guidance on carrying out assessments and treatment for children and young people with OCD from a cognitive behavioural perspective. This approach has been developed from extensive research and clinical work with young people with OCD and associated problems. The book includes:

- an overview of OCD
- an introduction to CBT and its relevance to OCD in young people
- assessment and treatment methods
- case studies and clinical vignettes
- worksheets for use with the client.

This straightforward text provides essential direction for practitioners and trainees in a range of professions including psychiatry, psychotherapy, counselling, nursing, education and social work.

Online resources:
The appendices of this book provide worksheets that can be downloaded free of charge to purchasers of the print version. Please visit the website www.routledgementalhealth. com/cbt-with-children to find out more about this facility.

Polly Waite is a Clinical Psychologist and Senior Research Fellow at the University of Reading.

Tim Williams is a Consultant Clinical Psychologist and Fellow in the Department of Psychology at the University of Reading.

CBT with Children, Adolescents and Families
Series editor: Paul Stallard

"The *CBT with Children, Adolescents and Families* series, edited by Professor Paul Stallard and written by a team of international experts, meets the growing need for evidence-based treatment manuals to address prevalent psychological problems in young people. These authoritative, yet practical books will be of interest to all professionals who work in the field of child and adolescent mental health." – *Alan Carr, Professor of Clinical Psychology, University College Dublin, Ireland*

Cognitive behaviour therapy (CBT) is now the predominant treatment approach in both the NHS and private practice and is increasingly used by a range of mental health professionals.

The *CBT with Children, Adolescents and Families* series provides comprehensive, practical guidance for using CBT when dealing with a variety of common child and adolescent problems, as well as related family issues. The demand for therapy and counselling for children and adolescents is rapidly expanding, and early intervention in family and school settings is increasingly seen as effective and essential. In this series leading authorities in their respective fields provide detailed advice on methods of achieving this.

Each book in this series focuses on one particular problem and guides the professional from initial assessment through to techniques, common problems and future issues. Written especially for the clinician, each title includes summaries of key points, clinical examples and worksheets to use with children and young people.

Titles in this series:

Anxiety by Paul Stallard
Obsessive Compulsive Disorder edited by Polly Waite and Tim Williams
Depression by Chrissie Verduyn, Julia Rogers and Alison Wood
Eating Disorders by Simon G. Gowers and Lynne Green
Post Traumatic Stress Disorder by Patrick Smith, Sean Perrin and William Yule

Obsessive Compulsive Disorder

Cognitive Behaviour Therapy with Children and Young People

Edited by
Polly Waite and Tim Williams

Routledge
Taylor & Francis Group

LONDON AND NEW YORK

First Published 2009
by Routledge
27 Church Road, Hove, East Sussex BN3 2FA

Simultaneously published in the USA and Canada
by Routledge
270 Madison Avenue, New York, NY 10016

Routledge is an imprint of the Taylor & Francis Group, an informa business

Typeset in Times by
RefineCatch Ltd, Bungay, Suffolk
Printed and bound in Great Britain by
TJ International Ltd, Padstow, Cornwall
Paperback cover design by Andy Ward

This publication has been produced with paper manufactured to strict
environmental standards and with pulp derived from sustainable forests.

British Library Cataloguing in Publication Data
A catalogue record for this book is available from the British Library

Library of Congress Cataloging-in-Publication Data
Obsessive compulsive disorder : cognitive behaviour therapy with children and
young people / edited by Polly Waite and Tim Williams.
    p. ; cm.
  Includes bibliographical references and index.
  1. Obsessive-compulsive disorder in children.   2. Obsessive-compulsive disorder in
adolescence.   3. Cognitive therapy for children.   4. Cognitive therapy for teenagers.
I. Waite, Polly, 1972–   II. Williams, Tim, 1955–.
  [DNLM: 1. Obsessive-Compulsive Disorder–therapy. 2. Adolescent. 3. Child.
4. Cognitive Therapy—methods. WM 176 O14268 2009]
  RJ506.O25O268 2009
  618.92′85227–dc22   20080226702

ISBN: 978–0–415–40388–7 (hbk)
ISBN: 978–0–415–40389–4 (pbk)

Contents

Figures

Contributors

Linda J. Atkinson Clinical Psychologist, Anxiety Disorders Residential Unit, Bethlem Royal Hospital, Alexandra House, Monks Orchard Road, Beckenham BR3 3BX, UK.

Dr Cathy Creswell Clinical Research Fellow, Winnicott Research Unit, Department of Psychology, University of Reading, Whiteknights, PO Box 238, Reading RG6 6AL, UK.

Dr Catherine Gallop Clinical Psychologist and Senior Teaching Fellow, University of Exeter, School of Psychology, Washington Singer, Perry Road, Exeter EX4 4QG, UK.

Professor Paul M. Salkovskis Professor of Clinical Psychology and Applied Science, Department of Psychology, Institute of Psychiatry, de Crespigny Park, Denmark Hill, London SE5 8AF and Clinical Director, Centre for Anxiety Disorders and Trauma, Maudsley Hospital, 99 Denmark Hill, London SE5 8AF, UK.

Blake Stobie Consultant Clinical Psychologist, Centre for Anxiety Disorders and Trauma, 99 Denmark Hill, London SE5 8AZ, UK.

Dr Polly Waite Clinical Psychologist and Senior Research Fellow, Department of Psychology, University of Reading, Whiteknights Road, Reading RG6 6AL, UK.

Dr Tim Williams Consultant Clinical Psychologist, Berkshire Healthcare NHS Trust and Fellow, Department of Psychology, University of Reading, Whiteknights Road, Reading RG6 6AL, UK.

Acknowledgements

We would like to thank all the contributors for their wholehearted support and hard work. We would also like to thank our other clinical colleagues, Dr Mark Allsopp, Prof Derek Bolton and Dr Sean Perrin and the Health Foundation, which brought us together to develop this work.

On a personal note, we would like to thank our families for their encouragement and support.

Finally, a special thank you to the young people and their families who have shared their experiences with us. It has been a privilege to work together and this book is dedicated to them.

1

Introduction to obsessive compulsive disorder

Tim Williams and Polly Waite

'OCD can be very stressful, not only affecting yourself but those around you. OCD meant that I felt I had to do habits in order to protect my family and myself. My OCD began when I was bullied at school, when my confidence was at its lowest, but the thing with OCD is that it itself is like a bully, eating away at your confidence.'

'When I had OCD I was miserable, depressed, worried, upset, felt out of place, alone and unloved. Some other feelings I had were that I was unpopular with people in and out of school. I felt I was stressed because of the thoughts in my head and routines I had done and that I struggled to do anything about it. I was very tired and very angry with myself and OCD.'

'Having OCD was restrictive and stressful. Because of the worries of having responsibility I was anxious and worried a lot of the time about bad things happening. I wouldn't really want to go out and at school I'd get conscious of "what if people notice?" I'd have to hide it but it was always there; there wasn't a break from it.'

These young people are telling us how it feels to be forced to do things again and again, and the worry that if these things are not done, something dreadful will happen. This is a common experience with obsessive compulsive disorder (OCD).

Diagnosis and characteristics of OCD in young people

In order to fulfil a diagnosis of OCD, an individual must experience either obsessions or compulsions. Obsessions are recurrent and persistent thoughts,

1

impulses or images (e.g. thoughts of becoming ill or images of a loved one dying) that are experienced at some time as intrusive and inappropriate and cause marked anxiety or distress (American Psychiatric Association, 1994). Consequently, the person attempts to ignore, suppress or neutralise them with some other thought or action.

Compulsions are repetitive behaviours (e.g. hand washing, ordering, checking) or mental acts (e.g. praying, counting, repeating words silently) that the person feels driven to perform in response to an obsession, or according to rules that must be applied rigidly (American Psychiatric Association, 1994). The aim of compulsions is to prevent or reduce distress or prevent a dreaded event or situation. However, they are not connected in a realistic way to the obsession or are clearly excessive. For example, a young person may experience an intrusive thought that they may suddenly become unpopular and rejected by their friends and carry out a compulsion of holding a good thought in their head, such as a memory of a happy time, in order to try to prevent the thought coming true. Many compulsions are visible to others and with young people, others (such as family members or teachers) may notice and become concerned about these behaviours before they are aware of any obsessions.

Although individuals often recognise that the obsessions or compulsions are excessive or unreasonable, in young people this is not necessary for a diagnosis. Finally, obsessions or compulsions must either cause marked distress, be time-consuming (taking more than an hour a day), or significantly interfere with their normal routine, academic or occupational functioning, or usual social activities or relationships (American Psychiatric Association, 1994).

> OCD is characterised by obsessive thoughts or compulsive behaviours which significantly interfere with everyday functioning.

Emily was a 15-year-old girl, who kept worrying that her parents or brother would become ill and die. This began two years ago, after a girl in her class died of leukaemia. Shortly before this, she could recall watching a television advert for a kitchen cleaner that showed brightly coloured germs spread everywhere. As a result, she avoided touching things that she felt other people would touch afterwards, like light switches and door handles, or if she did have to touch them she would try to use a tissue to limit possible contamination. She carried out compulsions, including excessive showering and washing her hands if she felt they were unclean or after touching anything she felt was 'germy'. She also described feeling contaminated if there was any mention of illness or death and would wash or shower herself to remove the sense of being contaminated. If she was unable to carry out compulsions or avoid contamination, she became extremely distressed that her thought of her family being ill or dying would come true and that she would have caused it.

Studies suggest that OCD in young people is characterised by a range of different types of obsessions and compulsions. The most common obsessions in young people include worries about dirt and contamination, thoughts of something terrible happening and concerns about illness or death (Thomsen, 1999). In younger children concerns about contamination, aggression and exactness or symmetry are most common (Franklin *et al.*, 1998; Geller *et al.*, 2001; Riddle *et al.*, 1990; Swedo *et al.*, 1989b). As children get older the types of obsessions may change to include obsessions of a sexual or religious nature. This is consistent with cognitive theories of OCD, which suggest that the content of obsessions reflects the issues that are important to the individual at that time (Salkovskis, 1985).

The most common compulsions in young people include washing, checking, repeating, ordering/arranging and counting (Thomsen, 1999). However, symptoms generally change over time and it is unusual for young people to only ever carry out one type of compulsion (Hanna, 1995; Rettew *et al.*, 1992; Wever and Rey, 1997). Swedo and Rapoport (1989) suggest that compulsions without obsessions are more common in childhood and that this may be because young children lack the cognitive ability to be able to articulate their internal cognitive processes. Compulsions without obsessions are frequently tactile (e.g. touching, tapping or rubbing rituals) and may occur more often in young people with a co-morbid tic disorder (Leckman *et al.*, 1995).

Research suggests that OCD has a significant impact on the lives of young people and their families. Allsopp and Verduyn (1988) suggest that childhood OCD is associated with significant disruption in academic, home and social functioning. In a study by Piacentini *et al.* (2003), around 90 per cent of young people participating reported that OCD affected their functioning in one area, while just under half reported significant OCD-related problems in each of the three areas assessed (school, home and socially). The two most common OCD-related problems were concentrating on schoolwork and doing homework. Impairment appeared to be associated with the severity of OCD symptoms, rather than factors such as age or gender.

- The most common obsessions include worries about dirt and contamination, thoughts of something terrible happening and concerns about illness or death.
- The most common compulsions in young people include washing, checking, repeating, ordering/arranging and counting.

Epidemiology

Research indicates that around 1 per cent of teenagers have OCD. Estimates of the prevalence and incidence in young people vary between 0.1 per cent and 4 per cent of the population across different countries (Flament *et al.*, 1988; Heyman *et al.*, 2001). There are no studies that have measured the prevalence in young people year on year and the majority of studies have been carried out with older children, not pre-pubertal children. Nevertheless, Heyman *et al.* (2001) suggest a continuing increase in numbers of cases from the age of 5 to 15 years. The variation in prevalence estimates may be accounted for by differences in diagnostic criteria, the methods of ascertainment (such as differences in the way interviews are conducted and whether they are conducted by clinicians or lay interviewers) and the motives of those taking part in the studies (for example, one of the higher estimates was found in a sample of teenage army recruits in Israel). In both the Flament *et al.* (1988) and Heyman *et al.* (2001) studies the majority of young people had not been diagnosed by clinical services and were not receiving treatment.

> Around 1 per cent of teenagers have OCD.

Age and triggers for onset

There appear to be two periods in life when OCD commonly begins, one around puberty, the second in early adulthood (Pauls *et al.*, 1995; Rasmussen and Eisen, 1992). This is likely to reflect developmental transitions to increasingly independent lifestyles. Although it is extremely rare, there have been cases of children as young as three or four years of age developing OCD.

OCD usually develops in a gradual way, but can also develop acutely, often in response to an adverse life event (Lensi *et al.*, 1996; Rachman and Hodgson, 1980). McKeon *et al.* (1984) found significantly more life events in the 12 months prior to the onset of the OCD, compared to a non-clinical control group. In our clinical experience, OCD in young people often appears to develop following bullying, difficulties with friends and illness or death within the family. Thomsen (1999) describes divorce and marital disharmony as significant, as well as triggering experiences such as illness or accidents.

> - In young people, OCD commonly begins around puberty, but can occur in children as young as three or four years of age.
> - Whilst it often develops in a gradual way, it can also develop acutely, often in response to an adverse life event.

Gender

Studies suggest that when OCD develops before puberty, boys outnumber girls by more than two to one (Geller *et al.*, 1998; Rasmussen and Eisen, 1992; Zohar, 1999). However, by the time young people reach adulthood, OCD affects men and women equally (Karno *et al.*, 1988), although there are differences in symptoms, with more women experiencing contamination fears and washing and cleaning compulsions and more men with obsessional slowness or sexual obsessions (Marks, 1987; Lensi *et al.*, 1996).

> When OCD develops before puberty, boys appear to outnumber girls, but by the time young people reach adulthood, there is no gender difference.

Seeking treatment

It appears that only around half of young people with OCD ask for any help (Flament *et al.*, 1988; Heyman *et al.*, 2001). The reasons for not seeking help are likely to include: a lack of awareness or understanding of the problem (by family members as well as young people); a fear that if the obsessional worry is verbalised this may increase the likelihood of it coming true; embarrassment; a fear of what others may think of them or how they may be treated and what might happen to them if they seek professional help. Many people with OCD report intense feelings of shame and humiliation due to the nature of their obsessive thoughts. They may often recognise that checking or washing will not in reality change anything, but feel powerless to stop. As a result, they may be less likely to seek help. On top of this, when individuals seek help they may not initially disclose information about the OCD (Torres *et al.*, 2007). This may be because the individual feels ashamed to report the nature of their symptoms or because professionals are not asking the right questions. Stobie *et al.* (2007) found that adults with OCD waited on average eight and a half years between their obsessional symptoms interfering significantly with their lives and being diagnosed.

> Only around half of young people with OCD ask for any help.

Raj was a 13-year-old boy, who described an incident where he had seen his younger sister in the bath and felt sexually aroused. After this, he became convinced that he might become a paedophile and specifically that he wanted to sexually abuse his sister. As a result, he tried desperately to try to push this thought out of his mind and prayed that he would be 'strong enough' not to carry out his thoughts. Because he felt he was on the brink of acting on them, he avoided being alone with his sister. He felt that he was a monster and was terribly ashamed of his thoughts. Although his family noticed him become depressed and more and more socially withdrawn, they were unsure why this was. He was unable to talk to any of his family members about it as he believed that they would be disgusted by him and not love him any more.

Course and prognosis

As treatment has evolved and improved over the years it is difficult to be clear about the natural course and outcome of OCD. Early follow-up studies suggested that the course of OCD was variable and that young people often experience a chronic but fluctuating course, with a waxing and waning of symptoms (Bolton *et al.*, 1995; Thomsen and Mikkelson, 1995). This is consistent with long-term follow-up studies with adults (e.g. Skoog and Skoog, 1999). However, there is reason to believe that as treatments improve, the prognosis is more hopeful. Stewart *et al.* (2004) completed a meta-analysis of follow-up studies. Not all studies involved treatment, and of those that did, treatment was variable and included CBT, psychotherapy, family therapy, medication, electroconvulsive therapy and even surgery. They found that 60 per cent of young people no longer met criteria for OCD with follow-ups of up to 15 years. However, it is difficult to be clear from this about the longitudinal course of untreated OCD or what factors predict a good outcome in treatment. They were able to identify factors that contributed to poorer outcomes and these included earlier age of onset, initial OCD severity, a longer duration of symptoms prior to diagnosis, the presence of a co-morbid tic or mood disorder and any family psychiatric history.

Wewetzer *et al.* (2001) followed up young people with OCD for an average of 11 years into adulthood. All the young people received either in-patient or outpatient treatment in specialist child and adolescent mental health services. Of the 36 per cent of young people who remained affected by OCD, over two-thirds had at least one further clinical disorder, such as anxiety or depression. Just over 70 per cent of all the young people continued to suffer from a mental health problem, including OCD, social phobia, depression, dysthymia and personality disorders.

> As treatment has evolved and improved over the years it is difficult to be clear about the natural course and outcome of OCD.

Differential diagnosis and co-morbidity

OCD is only one reason why children repeat actions. Young children below the age of ten years often have quite fixed routines and rituals at bedtime. For instance, children at this age may insist that their parents kiss them in particular ways or have a particular soft toy with them before the light is switched off. While very young children are unlikely to provide a clear reason for the rituals, older children may say that the soft toy or ritual prevents the appearance of monsters or other feared outcomes (see Troster, 1994; also Thelen, 1981). Children's games may also contain reasoning similar to that seen in OCD; for instance, children may sing 'Don't step on the cracks or the bogeyman will get you' while walking along a paved area. In this case, however, the fear is usually imaginary, rather than real. The key issue in understanding whether the behaviour is consistent with OCD is the degree to which the routines and rituals become dysfunctional and interfere with everyday life.

Another area of difficulty for the clinician is distinguishing OCD from stereotyped behaviour in children who have learning disabilities or autistic spectrum disorders. They may repeat actions for a number of other reasons such as the immediate pleasure of doing something well, or alleviating boredom rather than a feeling of preventing harm. In these instances, the ritual will be empty of meaning. However, people with autistic spectrum disorders can and do develop OCD so a careful description of the subjective experiences is necessary to determine the motivation behind the behaviour.

> A 13-year-old boy with Asperger's syndrome had developed a ritual of counting before he could open doors. When asked about this he explained that he had the feeling that something bad was going to happen if he did not open the door at just the right time. He was unable to identify a particular number that was involved, but he could explain that the anxiety or worrying thought came before he started to count. He also had other rituals such as getting dressed in a particular order which he described as being the right way to do things. These rituals he was able to modify under instruction, because they did not cause him distress. In this case, a diagnosis of OCD was made because he had the feeling that he had to do the counting ritual in order to prevent harm, whereas the dressing ritual seemed to be because he preferred to do things in a particular order.

Young people with OCD often have other psychological problems, with around 75 per cent experiencing difficulties that fulfil criteria for a diagnosis (March *et al.*, 2004; Swedo and Rapoport, 1989). This is not uncommon, as many other disorders have high rates of co-morbidity (Caron and Rutter, 1991). However, while anxiety and depression have a high rate of occurrence in OCD, it is less common to find OCD co-occurring with depression or anxiety, when they are the primary presenting problem (Shear *et al.*, 2006).

Other anxiety disorders are common in OCD, such as generalised anxiety (worries that are not related to the OCD and may be around school, friendships, family, world affairs), separation anxiety (usually being away from their parents) and social anxiety (worrying about social situations). The most recent British child mental health study (Heyman *et al.*, 2001) found that 52 per cent of young people with OCD had a co-morbid anxiety disorder. There is considerable overlap in the phenomenology of cognitions in OCD and worry and they may be intrusive, similar in form, occur repeatedly and be persistent (Comer *et al.*, 2004). Therefore it is unclear whether the co-morbidities reflect problems with the diagnostic systems or represent multiple pathologies. Nevertheless, the treatment of OCD with cognitive behaviour therapy (CBT) has a positive effect on other anxiety disorders (O'Kearney *et al.*, 2006).

The co-existence of depression or dysthymia in young people with OCD is not uncommon, with studies suggesting that up to 20 per cent of young people with OCD also have a mood disorder (Heyman *et al.*, 2001). It appears likely that this is often a secondary problem, as the OCD begins to have a significant impact on the young person's life. Whilst mild to moderate depression does not appear to have a significant impact on response to treatment, severe depression is associated with a poorer response (Abramowitz and Foa, 2000).

Young people with OCD may also experience externalising disorders, such as attention deficit hyperactivity disorder (ADHD), conduct disorder or oppositional defiant disorder. Different studies report different levels of co-morbidity, ranging between 10 per cent and 44 per cent (Heyman *et al.*, 2001; Swedo and Rapoport, 1989; Thomsen, 1999). This is likely to be influenced by both catchment populations and how the behaviour is classified. Many young people are in conflict with their parents as a result of the OCD and this presents difficulties in diagnosis, since the conflict may be a consequence of their OCD or it may be a separate problem indicating a more deep-seated difficulty, such as oppositional defiant disorder. ADHD is also found in clinic populations and may represent a particular difficulty for psychological treatment. Careful planning may be needed to maximise engagement and reduce the effects of impulsivity and poor attention.

Young people or families often have concerns that their obsessional worries are a sign of madness. However, delusions do not develop from obsessional thoughts (Rachman and Hodgson, 1980), nor is there a link between OCD and psychotic disorders more broadly (Salkovskis, 1996b). People with OCD generally have insight into their condition and recognise that their behaviour is irrational, whereas people with psychosis often lack insight.

There is evidence to suggest that tic disorders are linked to OCD. Nearly 50 per cent of young people with Tourette's syndrome (TS) also develop obsessional behaviours and higher rates of OCD have been found in first-degree relatives of people with TS (Leckman, 1993; Pauls *et al.*, 1995). However, it is unusual to see individuals with OCD developing tics later. The compulsions seen in TS are more likely to consist of touching, tapping, rubbing, blinking and staring rituals, with less ordering, cleaning and washing compulsions (Hanna *et al.*, 2002). It is likely that obsessional behaviours often develop as a secondary problem, in that as the individual anticipates a tic they may become anxious and carry out a ritual to reduce their anxiety.

> Up to 75 per cent of young people with OCD experience difficulties that fulfil criteria for additional diagnoses, such as anxiety disorders or depression.

Biological aspects of OCD

Heredity

The relative contributions of genes and the environment are not clearly understood. Studies suggest that in individuals with OCD, up to 10 per cent of their parents also meet criteria for a diagnosis (MacDonald *et al.*, 1992). Twin studies (e.g. Carey and Gottesman, 1981) suggest that there is a genetic component, but that it is an inheritance of a general predisposition to anxiety rather than OCD per se. Any genetic component appears to be quite small in comparison with other anxiety disorders (Eley *et al.*, 2003).

In recent years there has been an increasing emphasis in the research literature on the effects of parental mental health problems and their effects on the child. 'Top-down' studies have looked at the children of parents with OCD. Black *et al.* (2003) carried out a two-year follow-up study and demonstrated that although the children of parents with OCD were likely to go on to develop an emotional disorder, it was not particularly likely to be OCD. Other 'bottom-up' studies have investigated the parents of children with OCD and Derisley *et al.*'s (2005) study found that children with OCD were more likely to have parents with an anxiety disorder. Again there was little evidence of specificity of transmission. However, Hanna *et al.* (2005) identified higher rates of OCD in the close relatives of children with OCD than in the close relatives of children with no diagnosis. More distant relatives showed no higher an incidence of OCD, suggesting only a minor role for heredity.

> Although there appears to be a genetic component, this is quite small in comparison with other anxiety disorders and appears to be a general predisposition to anxiety, rather than OCD specifically.

Paediatric autoimmune neuropsychiatric disorder associated with streptococcal infection

Studies in the United States have drawn attention to the association between OCD and particular infections (Swedo *et al.*, 1998). Streptococcal bacteria, which typically cause sore throats, may trigger an autoimmune response in susceptible individuals (Snider and Swedo, 2004). Swedo and her colleagues have described five features which together indicate a paediatric autoimmune neuropsychiatric disorder associated with streptococcal infection (PANDAS): presence of OCD and/or a tic disorder, prepubertal age of onset, abrupt onset, a relapsing course, and association with neurological symptoms during exacerbations. While the range of symptoms does not differ from other early onset patients, the age of onset is earlier. In addition, the course of the disorder is characterised by sudden and severe deteriorations which remain for a few weeks before declining again. Preliminary indications are that a number of physical treatments such as particular antibiotics or therapeutic plasma exchange are effective in both treatment and prophylaxis (Snider and Swedo, 2004).

A recent quasi-epidemiological study found that 6 per cent of children with OCD had evidence of streptococcal infections within three months of the onset of the disorder (Mell *et al.*, 2005). This is three times more common than in children with no disorder but the rate of streptococcal infections in young people with other mental health problems is unknown and so we cannot be sure how specific the link is.

> Further research is required to detail the specific link between streptococcal infections and OCD.

Neuropsychology

Given that young people report problems with decision-making and memory, it is not surprising that researchers have proposed that there may be cognitive deficits in OCD. Although there is little research on neuropsychological functioning in young people with OCD, there have been studies of neuropsychological functioning in adult populations. This suggests that OCD may be characterised by executive deficits (which includes abilities such organisation, planning and shifting from one way of thinking or rule to another), attention and memory difficulties and visuospatial and visuoconstructional impairments (e.g. Aronowitz *et al.*, 1994; Boone *et al.*, 1991; Christensen *et al.*, 1992; Head *et al.*, 1989). However, much of this research has been carried out on non-clinical or subclinical samples, sample sizes are often small and many studies do not include normal or clinical (especially anxious) control groups. In addition, studies have struggled to find associations between specific cognitive deficits and actual symptom subtypes, such as memory difficulties in compulsive checkers, or a relationship between impairments and symptom severity.

An alternative to the cognitive deficit theory is that patients try too hard to control their cognitive functioning and consequently other cognitive functions suffer as a result of competition for processing resources (Salkovskis,

1996a). Radomsky *et al.* (2001) suggested that the development and persistence of OCD may be related to a lack of confidence in memory rather than deficits in memory and found that young people with OCD had less confidence in their memory only for threat-relevant material under a high responsibility condition. Cougle *et al.* (in press) also found that checkers performed similarly to a non-clinical control group in their recall of actions and that their accuracy of recall was correlated with their confidence in memory. They hypothesised that there may be a high level of concern about making a mistake and so checking then becomes a way of trying to be sure that they have not caused harm.

Brain structure and chemistry

Biological accounts of OCD have sought to explain OCD in terms of general deficits in specific areas of the brain or in differences in neurotransmitters. Studies have focused particularly on serotonin, the neurotransmitter that is known to modulate mood, emotion, sleep and appetite and is implicated in the control of numerous behavioural and physiological functions. The finding that particular medications which act as serotonin reuptake inhibitors (SSRIs) can be effective in reducing OCD symptoms led to the initial hypothesis that there may be an abnormality in serotonin and studies have reported different levels of serotonin in OCD (e.g. Insel *et al.*, 1985; Zohar *et al.*, 1988). In addition, brain scanning studies have been used to suggest that there are biological differences in OCD, such as differing metabolic rates in the part of the brain known as the fronto-striatal system (e.g. Baxter *et al.*, 1988). However, just because differences are found does not necessarily mean that there is a deficit or abnormality. Baxter *et al.* (1992) demonstrated that the anomalies detected through brain scanning can resolve through medication or behaviour therapy, suggesting that any neurological changes are reversible.

If OCD is caused by biological factors, theories need to be able to account for the effectiveness of treatment and to explain how psychological therapy may work. Theories must also be able to account for the phenomenology of OCD more broadly, such as why memory and decision-making problems only occur in situations linked to the obsessional problem. To progress our understanding, biological accounts of OCD need to be able to generate specific predictions based on the phenomenology of OCD and must be able to provide evidence to evaluate them.

Biological theories have been very influential in the literature on OCD. However, biological approaches have lacked well-elaborated theories and have struggled to account for the phenomena of OCD.

Psychological aspects of OCD

Causes

Salkovskis *et al.* (1999) have suggested five mechanisms for the development of inflated responsibility which they propose are critical for the development of OCD. These include:

- being given too much responsibility
- being given too little responsibility
- exposure to rigid or extreme codes of conduct
- incidents where that person's action or inaction contributed to serious misfortune
- incidents where the person erroneously assumed that their thoughts, actions or inactions contributed to a serious misfortune.

As Salkovskis *et al.* (1999) point out, these factors are unlikely to be the sole causes of developing OCD. Personal vulnerabilities such as sensitivity to criticism or negative events are also likely to play a part. As yet there have been no studies exploring these mechanisms in young people with OCD.

Family functioning

For many families coping with their child's OCD is a strain. The symptoms of OCD may affect the living arrangements at home or the capacity of the family to go out together. For instance, if the young person is unable to leave the house without spending half an hour in the bathroom, then the morning routine of getting ready to go to work or school may be disrupted. It may be that the young person is unable to complete tasks without asking the parents for reassurance that the tasks have indeed been completed correctly or they may get parents to carry out compulsions for them, such as turning out the bedroom light before going to sleep. Recent studies have suggested that there are particular issues which differentiate families of children with OCD from those that have children with other types of problem. Barrett *et al.* (2002) found that parents of children with OCD were less confident in their children's abilities and independence skills than parents of children with other anxiety disorders and were less likely to use positive problem-solving techniques. Derisley *et al.* (2005) found that parents of children with OCD tended to cope with problems by avoiding them.

However, research on the best way of helping families overcome these difficulties is still at an early stage. There are not yet any studies comparing individual CBT with CBT involving families in young people with OCD. However, Barrett *et al.* (2004) obtained greater effect sizes using family CBT than the effect sizes in the paediatric OCD treatment study (POTS) trial (March *et al.*, 2004). Where comparative studies have been carried out in anxiety disorders more generally, the picture is unclear; for example,

Cobham *et al.* (1998) only found limited benefits in involving parents in the intervention.

> Research on family involvement is still at an early stage and so far studies on anxiety disorders more generally have found limited benefits in involving parents in therapy.

Behavioural models of OCD

Behavioural theories of OCD stem from Mowrer's (1960) two-factor theory of the development of anxiety, which involves both classical and operant conditioning. Obsessions are previously neutral stimuli which have become associated with anxiety. The individual then develops avoidance and escape responses, such as washing or checking, that terminate exposure to the feared stimulus. The behaviours are negatively reinforced, which makes them more likely to occur and termination of exposure prevents the anxiety from extinguishing (Rachman, 1971).

Behavioural treatments of OCD

Behavioural accounts led to the development of exposure and response prevention (ERP) as a psychological treatment for OCD (Meyer, 1966; Rachman *et al.*, 1971). This involves encouraging the individual to expose themselves to the thoughts, situations or activities that induce anxiety for a prolonged period of time, without carrying out the compulsion or other responses that normally terminate the exposure. As a result, they learn to tolerate the anxiety or discomfort, over time the anxiety decreases and through repetition it eventually habituates. In addition, they may discover that the feared consequence does not occur.

Early studies in adults demonstrated that ERP was a successful treatment (Meyer *et al.*, 1974; Rachman and Hodgson, 1980); around 60 to 70 per cent of individuals with compulsions who completed treatment made significant improvements (Abramowitz, 1996). However, behavioural treatments have been difficult to apply to young people who ruminate or do not have compulsions and treatment refusal and drop-outs have been common. There has been one randomised controlled trial of ERP in young people (Bolton and Perrin, 2008), which found that ERP reduced OCD symptoms substantially as compared with a waiting list condition.

> Psychological interventions for OCD began in the 1960s with the development of ERP and this led to reasonable success with adults and later with young people.

Cognitive theories of OCD

Most cognitive accounts of OCD have developed from Rachman and de Silva's (1978) finding that almost 90 per cent of a non-clinical sample reported intrusive thoughts that were no different to the obsessional thoughts experienced in OCD. This finding has been subsequently replicated and more recently there is evidence to suggest that compulsions do not differ in content to normal ritualistic behaviour (Fiske and Haslam, 1997; Muris *et al.*, 1997). These findings suggest that the basic phenomenon involved in OCD is extremely common.

Salkovskis (1985) hypothesised that the key difference between people with and without OCD is the way in which the intrusive thoughts are interpreted, both in terms of their occurrence and content. In individuals without OCD, intrusive thoughts are generally not interpreted as being meaningful and as a result they are able to dismiss them. However, in individuals with OCD the thoughts are seen as an indication that they might be responsible for harm to themselves or others unless they take action to prevent it. Responsibility appraisals are defined as 'the belief that one has power which is pivotal to bring about or prevent subjectively crucial negative outcomes'. Consequently, the individual attempts to suppress and neutralise the thought through compulsions, avoidance of situations related to the thought, seeking reassurance or by attempting to get rid of the thought. The aim of these neutralising behaviours is to reduce the perceived responsibility. However, they actually make further intrusive thoughts more meaningful and more likely to occur, evoke more discomfort and lead to further neutralising.

Rachman (1997, 1998, 2003) extends the cognitive theory to suggest that in OCD, individuals catastrophically misinterpret the significance of their normal intrusive thoughts and this causes obsessions. For an intrusive thought to become an obsession, it must be misinterpreted as important, personally significant, contrary to the individual's value system and having potential and serious consequences (even if it is perceived to be unlikely). Obsessions then persist as neutralisation and avoidance stop the individual finding out that the perceived consequence does not occur. Certain cognitive biases can then increase the significance of obsessional thinking, such as thought–action fusion or inflated responsibility. Thought–action fusion involves the individual regarding the obsessional thought as being morally equivalent to carrying out the action (e.g. having a thought of harming someone is as bad as actually doing it) and/or feeling that having the thought increases the likelihood of it coming true (Rachman and Shafran, 1998). Responsibility beliefs may also contribute to catastrophically misinterpreting intrusive thoughts and may be a cause or effect of thought–action fusion.

In 1995, a group of international researchers agreed to collaborate to develop and evaluate measures of cognition in OCD. Known as the Obsessive Compulsive Cognitions Working Group (OCCWG), they reached a consensus about the key cognitions in OCD, identifying six major belief domains that they believed were significant in OCD (OCCWG, 1997). These were:

- *inflated responsibility* – the belief that one has power which is pivotal to bring about or prevent subjectively crucial negative outcomes
- *over-importance of thought* – the belief that the presence of an intrusive thought indicates that it is important
- *overestimation of threat* – an exaggeration in the estimation of the probability or severity of harm
- *the controllability of thoughts* – the belief that it is possible, desirable and necessary to control thoughts
- *intolerance of uncertainty* – the belief that it is necessary to be certain and that it will be impossible to cope without complete certainty
- *perfectionism* – the belief that there is a perfect solution to every problem, that doing something perfectly is not only possible but also necessary, and that even minor mistakes will have serious consequences.

Some of these cognitions appear to be specific to OCD, such as inflated responsibility, while others such as perfectionism are relevant to OCD but also occur commonly in other disorders.

Cognitions in young people with OCD

There is evidence to suggest that young people in general also experience intrusive thoughts that are no different to those experienced in OCD and that if the thoughts cause distress and/or are more actively managed, they tend to persist for longer (Allsopp and Williams, 1996). Studies comparing young people with OCD to non-anxious controls or young people with other anxiety disorders have sought to investigate whether the same belief domains shown in adults with OCD are present in younger populations. Libby *et al.* (2004) found that young people with OCD had significantly more responsibility appraisals and beliefs around thought–action fusion than anxious controls. Barrett and Healy (2003) also found inflated responsibility and increased thought–action fusion and higher ratings of harm severity in young people with OCD but that the differences were not significant. This may reflect differences in measures used, or it may be that as this was with a younger sample cognitions may not be fully developed. Nevertheless, they did find the group of young people with OCD were significantly different when it came to cognitive control. This provides some preliminary evidence that young people with OCD demonstrate similar cognitions identified in adults with OCD.

> Cognitive accounts of OCD suggest that intrusive thoughts are experienced by most of the population and that the key difference between people with and without OCD is the way in which the intrusive thoughts are interpreted in terms of their occurrence and content.

Cognitive behaviour therapy for OCD

Cognitive behaviour therapy (CBT) for OCD developed as an attempt to increase adherence to ERP, by helping the individual to modify dysfunctional thoughts and beliefs (Salkovskis and Warwick, 1985). However, as theoretical and empirical studies on cognitions in OCD developed, CBT has evolved as a treatment in its own right. It is based on modifying key beliefs and appraisals so that the individual learns that intrusive thoughts are not of special significance and do not indicate increased responsibility or probability of harm. CBT aims to help the individual to construct and test a new and less threatening model of their experience through developing an understanding of how the problem may be working and then testing this out through behavioural experiments to learn that the problem is about thinking and worry, rather than actual danger or harm. Whereas in ERP the individual is encouraged to stop carrying out compulsions, in CBT the individual is encouraged to carry out experiments to identify and challenge their misinterpretations. As a result, they learn that they no longer need to carry out compulsions.

It is clear that CBT is effective in significantly reducing symptoms of OCD and that these gains are maintained post-treatment (Clark, 2004). There is evidence that it is effective with symptoms that have been more difficult to treat with ERP, such as obsessional ruminations and hoarding (Freeston *et al.*, 1997; Hartl and Frost, 1999). More recently, controlled trials with adults have compared CBT to ERP and found CBT to be superior to ERP in reducing symptom severity and shifting obsessional beliefs (Rector *et al.*, 2006; Salkovskis *et al.*, in press).

CBT with young people and families

A number of studies of CBT with young people have been carried out. One of the earliest controlled studies demonstrated that CBT was as effective as clomipramine for the control of the symptoms of OCD (de Haan *et al.*, 1998). Subsequent studies have compared CBT with waiting list controls (Bolton and Perrin, 2008), with sertraline (Asbahr *et al.*, 2005; March *et al.*, 2004) and have delivered CBT in family (Barrett *et al.*, 2004) or group formats (Asbahr *et al.*, 2005). All of the CBT programmes have produced similar improvements in measures of OCD. Nevertheless, there are differences between the approaches adopted. Most forms of CBT have focused on encouraging the young person to manage the anxiety or discomfort associated with ERP (e.g. see March and Mulle, 1998). In this book we describe a different approach which encourages the young person to find out for themselves how their thinking is the problem rather than their behaviour and draws on the developments made in the adult field. There are no direct comparisons of this approach with others.

> CBT is based on modifying key beliefs and appraisals with the aim of helping the individual to construct and test a new and less threatening model of their experience.

The role of medication

Studies suggest that serotonin reuptake inhibitors are effective in treating young people with OCD (e.g. Flament *et al.*, 1985; Leonard *et al.*, 1989; March and Mulle, 1998). Geller *et al.* (2003) completed a meta-analysis of pharmacotherapy trials in young people with OCD and found clomipramine to be more effective than four newer selective serotonin reuptake inhibitors (SSRIs). However, the side effects from clomipramine mean that it is no longer widely used. There was no significant difference between the newer SSRIs and overall medication appeared to be reasonably effective for around 60 per cent of young people. However, there are concerns that antidepressant medication may increase suicidality and consequently the advice in the UK is to carefully monitor potential adverse outcomes. A significant problem with medication is the relapse rate and consequently the National Institute for Health and Clinical Excellence (NICE) guidelines (2005) for the UK suggest long-term use.

The paediatric OCD treatment study (POTS) randomised controlled trial (March *et al.*, 2004) compared medication, CBT and a combination of medication and CBT. They found that the young people treated with CBT alone or in combination with medication showed the greatest improvement, although medication alone was better than a placebo. However, it has not yet been established who benefits from which treatment.

> There is an evidence base for the use of medication with young people. However, CBT alone or in combination with medication appears to be more effective and less likely to lead to relapse.

Choice of treatment

The consensus guidelines produced by the American Psychiatric Association (March *et al.*, 1997) suggested that CBT was the first choice treatment for children and young people. More recently, NICE described a stepped care model beginning with self-help materials for mild cases through to CBT, medication and finally combined treatments (NICE, 2005). However, self-help materials for young people with OCD are not readily available and have not been evaluated. Consequently, it is not clear how effective they are. There is a danger that by beginning with interventions that do not have an adequate evidence base we are delaying the young person receiving effective treatment and this may lead to additional problems, such as symptoms increasing in frequency and severity, as well as leading the young person, family and professionals to believe that the problem is difficult to treat.

> When deciding what treatment should be used in treating OCD, the general consensus is for a stepped care approach with CBT as a first line treatment.

2

The use of CBT with children and adolescents

Cathy Creswell and Polly Waite

Introduction

CBT is based on the general notion that a psychological disorder is caused or maintained by 'dysfunctional' patterns of thoughts and behaviours (e.g. Beck *et al.*, 1979). That is, the disorder is conceptualised as resulting at least in part from the individual's cognitive distortions (such as false attributions or expectations about the self, others or the world) that then undermine positive coping or problem-solving behaviour. CBT has its roots in behaviour therapy, which applies learning theory to psychological problems; for example, using 'exposure' to overcome avoidance of anxiety-provoking stimuli, and 'response prevention' to minimise compulsive behaviours. To date many CBT treatments with younger populations have been predominantly behavioural in content. Recently, however, there have been exciting developments in the understanding of cognitive aspects of psychological problems in childhood. In addition, recent models have begun to incorporate the maintaining role of environmental influences. For example, in Rapee's (2001) model of the development of generalised anxiety disorder (GAD), parental reaction and factors associated with socialisation are hypothesised to promote the expression of anxious vulnerability in young people. As cognitive and behavioural models of childhood disorder become further refined, so will treatments, leading to greater specificity of treatments to particular disorders and a clearer understanding of how best to include families in treatment.

> CBT is based on the idea that psychological problems are maintained by unhelpful patterns of thinking and behaviour.

Developmental issues in CBT

In order to benefit from CBT for OCD, young people need to be able: (a) to distinguish between thoughts, feelings and behaviours; (b) to reflect on their own cognitive processes; (c) to understand the relationship between cause and effect. It appears that the majority of children can demonstrate these skills by seven or eight years of age (Salmon and Bryant, 2002). For example, Quakley *et al.* (2004) presented children with a thought–feeling–behaviour sorting task and whilst four-year-old children performed at a level that did not differ from chance, by seven years of age most children performed at the ceiling level. Interestingly, at younger ages using a glove puppet to present the task improved performance, highlighting the need for careful consideration not only of *what* we do in therapy, but also *how* we do it to maximise children's engagement and understanding. In terms of reflecting on thoughts, or 'thinking about thinking', a number of studies have demonstrated that pre-school children can attribute different thoughts to different people. By five years of age they can use mental state terms to explain behaviours, and by eight years to explain feelings (see Grave and Blissett, 2005). In terms of causal reasoning, again pre-school children are able to accurately use internal states to inform reasoning, and furthermore are able to consider 'counter-factuals'; in other words, what if something different happens next time they are in this situation? Again though, studies have highlighted the importance of how these questions are asked in younger children (Robinson and Beck, 2000).

Does the basic cognitive model apply to children?

Research over the last decade has shown that characteristic cognitions are associated with particular mood disorders, including anxiety (Barrett *et al.*, 1996b), depression (Abela *et al.*, 2002) and conduct disorder (Crick and Dodge, 1994) in young people, largely mirroring those cognitive patterns found in adult populations. For example, in comparison to adolescents (11–18 years) with other anxiety disorders and non-anxious participants, adolescents with OCD have been found to have inflated responsibility beliefs, increased thought–action fusion (the idea that having a thought of something bad happening increases the likelihood of the event occurring) and concern over mistakes (Libby *et al.*, 2004). An integral relationship between cognitive style and OCD is also supported by a case series of six adolescents where measures of inflated responsibility decreased as OCD symptoms decreased (Williams *et al.*, 2002). Among younger children, these characteristic cognitive styles may not be fully developed. For example, in a younger sample, children (aged 7 to 13 years) with OCD also reported inflated responsibility and increased thought–action fusion in comparison to other anxious and non-anxious children, as well as the highest ratings of harm severity (that is, how bad it would be if the feared consequence happened). However, these were not statistically significant differences. The only domain that significantly differentiated the OCD group clearly from the other groups was that of cognitive control, in that the OCD group indicated that they were less able to stop themselves worrying about a thought than the others (Barrett and Healy, 2003).

There is also some evidence that levels of magical thinking – that is, the attribution of causal effects on real events by a thought or action that is physically unconnected to the event – are associated with obsessive compulsive symptoms in young people between the ages of five and 17 (Bolton *et al.*, 2002; Muris *et al.*, 2001). However, further research is required to establish whether this relationship exists in young people who fulfil criteria for a diagnosis of OCD and if it is specific to OCD.

Together, these studies provide initial evidence for a cognitive account of OCD in young people. However, the reliance of studies to date on samples representing broad age ranges means we do not know whether these cognitive styles are present in both young and older children. Our reliance on data from cross-sectional studies also limits the conclusions that can be drawn about the direction of the association between cognitions, behaviour and affect in OCD. For example, it is unlikely that intrusive thoughts will present a problem or drive compulsive behaviour until a young person has developed the ability to reflect on thoughts and their meaning. Indeed, it is widely recognised that intrusive thoughts are experienced by the majority of people (e.g. Rachman and de Silva, 1978). So does OCD in youth represent a failure to learn to disregard these normal intrusive phenomena? If so, why do some children fail to go through this otherwise normative process of development?

CBT models for adult populations are focused largely on the maintenance cycles, based on the premise that maladaptive thinking styles have developed during childhood which are no longer adaptive in the adult's life (e.g. Beck *et al.*, 1979). When working with younger populations it is important to establish whether these beliefs continue to serve an adaptive function in the child's life. For example, it is essential to consider the wider environmental influences that will be affecting the young person's thoughts, behaviour and mood. However, the specific influences on the development of cognitions and behaviour associated with OCD in childhood are not well understood. Salkovskis *et al.* (1999) argue that the origins of obsessional problems are likely to be the result of complex interactions specific to the individual, but that there are likely to be a number of different pathways to the development of beliefs around inflated responsibility (see Chapter 1). Prospective, experimental and treatment studies are all urgently needed to provide a better understanding of the specific environmental influences on OCD in young people and the relative importance of these, cognitions and behaviours in order for us to know the crucial elements to target within therapy.

- Similar cognitive styles have been identified in children and adults with OCD. However it is not yet clear whether the *nature* of the relationship between cognitions, affect and behaviour is the same throughout development.
- The specific influences on the development of cognitions and behaviour associated with OCD in childhood are not well understood and further research is necessary.

An overview of CBT with young people

A cornerstone of the practice of CBT is *collaboration* between the therapist and the client, whether that client is an adult or a young person (or a family). The therapist is *working with the young person*. The therapist is not 'the expert' but all the different parties are bringing together their particular areas of expertise to overcome the problem. This approach is crucial when working with young people with difficulties including depression, anxiety and specifically OCD, where cognitions are commonly characterised by self-doubt. For this reason therapy needs to be delivered in a way that *promotes the young person's self-efficacy and perceived control*. This approach is also essential from a practical point of view. Due to the resource limitations that face services it is essential that therapy promotes the development of skills that can continue to be used over time, independently from the therapist and enable the young person to deal effectively with any future setbacks that may occur once therapy has come to an end.

There are a number of key features in delivering CBT that meet these theoretical and practical demands, which will be reviewed briefly below. First, however, we should acknowledge that when working with young people, in contrast to adults, it is extremely unlikely that the young person will be the one who has sought help. In most cases it will be a parent or carer, or in some cases a teacher or other adult. For treatment to work, the young person needs to play their part and so it is important to consider their *motivation to change* right from the start. A common method in helping the young person is to identify the pros and cons of having OCD and the pros and cons of changing how things are. Young people may need prompting to consider longer term considerations. Even when long-term factors have been taken into account, particularly for pre-adolescents, they may not be weighed as heavily as immediate or short-term factors. For this reason it is necessary to make sure that the current environment promotes change and this may involve working with parents to ensure that they are reinforcing the young person to take risks and be brave in order to overcome their problem. Equally, motivation to change and engagement in therapy should be regularly reviewed as the young person is unlikely to complain during the therapy sessions, but instead will simply refuse to come back. This can be addressed directly with the young person but also signs of withdrawal from the therapist or the therapy process should be picked up and discussed openly at the earliest opportunity. Allowing the young person to express both the things they like and dislike will allow the therapist and young person to consider ways of making the therapy more acceptable. For example, should the sessions be shorter? Should they take place somewhere else? Should someone else attend too?

- CBT should be delivered in a collaborative way that promotes the young person's sense of self-efficacy and control.
- It is crucial to consider the young person's motivation to change right from the start and therapy may need to address this in order to be successful.
- It is important that the environment is set up to promote change and this is likely to involve working with family members.

Structure of sessions

A basic but often neglected starting point is making sure that sessions have a clear structure and a set agenda. This is crucial from a practical point of view as the number of sessions that are available will generally be time-limited. The young person will also feel more in control of the content of sessions if they are predictable in structure and everyone's items are set on the agenda for discussion. Agendas need to be set so that they are not overly ambitious and allow for repetition and practice of ideas. If the young person does not have items to actually add, at the very least they can dictate where the session should start. At times, family members may have different agendas, which the therapist will need to address without losing sight of the young person's needs. It may be possible to deal with different agendas within sessions or it may be necessary to organise separate sessions for family members.

- Sessions should have a clear structure and agenda.
- If family members have different agendas, the therapist will need to address this and may need to organise separate sessions.

The basic tools

The key tools in CBT are:

1   Developing a joint formulation.

2   Psychoeducation to make sense of the maintaining role of thoughts and behaviours.
3   Guided discovery using Socratic questioning.
4   Guided discovery using behavioural experiments.
5   Relapse prevention.

Developing a joint formulation

This describes the process of working with the young person to achieve a shared understanding of what is keeping the problem going. By definition, this formulation needs to be worked out explicitly with the young person: for example, using a large piece of paper or a flip chart and making sure the young person has a pen in their hand throughout so that they are free to write or draw as much as they wish.

For the young person to feel ownership of this formulation, it needs to be described entirely using their terms: for example, if they or the family have a particular name that is used to refer to OCD, or whether there is a picture image associated with it. Indeed, using pictures to illustrate the formulation can make it both livelier and more meaningful.

Formulations for OCD must pay specific attention not just to automatic thoughts but also to the meaning of these thoughts and how they then relate to feelings and behaviours. For example, the thought that 'My Mum could get knocked down crossing a road on her way to work' may be frightening enough, but may also be associated with other thoughts about what this means; for example, 'If I don't do a compulsion, it will be my fault if it happens.' Even in cases where the presentation appears predominantly behavioural (i.e. compulsions) there are still likely to be associated cognitions that are maintaining the disorder, for example, a belief that they will be overwhelmed by distress if the compulsion is not performed. To elicit these it will be necessary to ask, for example, 'What would you worry deep down would happen if you didn't do X?' or 'In your worst nightmare, what would happen if you weren't able to do X?' Examples of formulations are given in Chapters 4 to 7. Typically, the therapist and young person regularly revisit the formulation in subsequent sessions as they acquire more information through discussion and behavioural experiments.

- A shared formulation, written down in the young person's terms, is a way of making sense of the problem.

- It enables the young person to see how the problem has evolved and why it keeps going.

Psychoeducation

In order to help the therapist and young person to develop an idiosyncratic explanation of what is maintaining the symptoms, it is useful to help them to recognise the role that thoughts and beliefs can play in determining feelings and behaviour. Seeing from the outset that it is perfectly normal for our thoughts to take on this role can help young people (and their families) to view their behaviours as quite understandable, rather than being weird or a sign of madness. This also provides an opportunity to be creative and allow the young person to have fun within the therapeutic environment. Cartoons can be readily employed to illustrate different ways of interpreting scenarios, as can reference to television programmes, for example, soap operas where characters endlessly misinterpret situations and create problems for themselves. Figure 2.1 illustrates one way of playing a family game to demonstrate associations between thoughts, feelings and behaviour. This particular example could be used with a young person who had worries and compulsions that are not around contamination as the point is to pick something that is unrelated to the young person's OCD. This example can engage young people as it is quite silly and different reactions appear odd when people do not know what is written on each other's cards.

Commonly in OCD, it is the meanings attributed to intrusive thoughts that are critical to the emergence and maintenance of anxiety and avoidant and compulsive behaviours. Consequently, providing information about the frequency and content of intrusive thoughts in the general population serves an essential normalising function. In addition, imagery, metaphor and narratives can all be used to illustrate other key concepts, for example, the repetition of behaviours as attempts to prevent harm. This will be discussed in greater detail in following chapters.

The therapist describes a scenario to the family, e.g. 'It is your first day at school. You have your new school uniform on and have spent quite a long time making sure you look good. You walk out of your front door and tread right in a dog poo!' The therapist then writes a number of different interpretations of this scenario on different pieces of paper and hand them round the room to each family member. For example:

- Everyone will think I stink and not want to be my friend.
- That dog did that on purpose.
- It's good luck to tread in dog poo.
- That dog has had a problem with its bowels and has been in lots of pain because it hasn't been able to poo for weeks.

The therapist then asks each family member to tell the rest of the group how they would feel and what they would do in this situation, before revealing what is on their piece of paper. Discuss with the family how the exact same scenario can be interpreted in such different ways, which lead to quite different feelings and behaviours.

Figure 2.1   Thoughts, feelings and behaviour game

- Psychoeducation is crucial in starting to generate a different way of making sense of the problem.

- With OCD in particular, information about how common intrusive thoughts are in the normal population is an essential part of therapy.

Guided discovery

Guided discovery refers to the process of helping a young person to consider other points of view and put alternative thoughts or beliefs to the test. A variety of techniques can be used to achieve this goal and these need not be limited to techniques traditionally associated with cognitive therapy as long as the choice of strategy is based on the case formulation and the goals of the particular session. Socratic questioning and behavioural experiments are, however, central to cognitive therapy so will be reviewed briefly here.

Socratic questioning

Socratic questioning is a way of asking questions to explore beliefs and assumptions, to uncover issues and problems and to work through the logical implications of beliefs. Rather than directly challenging a young person's interpretations and thoughts, the therapist works with the young person asking questions to examine thoughts, test their validity and utility and examine alternatives. Typical questions that are used with adults can also be used with young people and some examples are given in Figure 2.2.

- What sense do you make of what happened?
- What do you think caused it to happen?
- If you were to repeat it, do you think you would get the same results?
- What do you think that means?
- What would be an alternative?
- Is there another way to look at it?
- Which explanation fits best with what happened?
- How does this tie in with what we learned before?
- What does this mean generally?
- How does this apply to everyday life?
- What does this mean for the future?

Figure 2.2   Examples of Socratic questioning

As the young person answers the questions, the therapist listens and reflects, summarises what they have heard and asks the young person further questions to think about the new information in relation to their original belief. The young person is more likely to believe a new way of thinking if it is based on information they have provided rather than information provided by the therapist.

The tone in which these questions are asked is the key to their success. If a young person feels as if they are being asked a question to which the therapist has a 'right' answer in mind, they will feel like they are being tested or are somehow wrong or silly to think as they do. Instead the questions must be asked genuinely out of curiosity with no desired outcome in mind. The purpose of the questioning is to help the young person to consider different ways of thinking.

When considering the evidence for particular beliefs, it is helpful to ask the young person to consider whether they have had any experiences that have showed that their belief is not true or when they are not feeling anxious whether they think about it in a different way. In our experience, young people often find it helpful to consider different ways of thinking when it is in reference to a different person doing the thinking, for example, 'What would your friend X think if this happened to them?' With younger children, the use of characters from stories or television programmes may help them to be able to consider a different perspective (see Figure 2.3).

It may be necessary to use prompts or make tentative suggestions to help a young person to answer these questions. At times, however, the young person may respond with 'I don't know'. If this is the case, the job of the therapist and young person is to work out how we could get to know the answer. This is one role of behavioural experiments.

- The therapist works with the young person to explore their beliefs and assumptions and examine alternatives through Socratic questioning.
- They are encouraged to think about the evidence for their old belief versus an alternative viewpoint.

---

1 Imagine you are (a crime-busting character that the young person knows) and you want to know if this thought is true. What is the evidence that it is true? What is the evidence that it isn't true?

2 If the same thing happened to (a friend), what would they think? Why would they think it had happened?

3 If this same thing happened to (a friend), what would you tell them?

Figure 2.3 Questioning beliefs

Behavioural experiments

The purpose of behavioural experiments is to test thoughts to assess their validity and utility. This can be necessary when there is not enough available evidence to fully evaluate a thought, or when the available evidence is just not convincing to the young person ('I know I shouldn't think it, but I still do' or 'I know it, but I don't feel it'). Experiments must have a clear hypothesis to be tested and alternative explanations for possible results need to be taken into account from the start, so that the results cannot be discounted after the experiment has taken place. Following the experiment, the results need to be considered with explicit reference to the initial thought being tested.

There are various types of behavioural experiments, ranging from active experiments, such as real situations or role play, to observational experiments, such as the young person observing the therapist performing an experiment, carrying out surveys or gathering information from other sources.

In OCD, active experiments are essential for challenging the young person's beliefs, such as the likelihood of harm occurring or to test the idea that thinking something can make it happen. Historically, exposure and response prevention (ERP) has been used to treat OCD, where the young person is encouraged to experience the intrusive thought without carrying out the compulsion. For example, if the young person is worried about contamination, they may be encouraged to touch a door handle without then washing their hands. With a more cognitive approach, ERP may still be used but this would always be specifically as a behavioural experiment to test out a particular cognition. For example, if the young person's belief is 'If I touch the door handle without washing my hands I could get ill', then the experiment may involve ERP. However, if the belief is 'If I touch the door handle, I will be so anxious that I will go mad', then the experiment may involve the young person touching the door handle and then allowing a sufficient amount of time to pass so that they are able to learn that the anxiety eventually remits. In this case, they could wash their hands afterwards without affecting the outcome of the experiment. Rather than designing a graded hierarchy of exposure tasks for the young person to work through, behavioural experiments are set up as a way of finding out how the world really works, and as a result they are designed in an idiosyncratic way according to the young person's beliefs. Other information such as that provided by surveys can also be helpful to find out that other people have intrusive thoughts, to consider how often other people are able to achieve perfection or a 'just right' feeling or to find out about other people's experiences of anxiety.

As much as possible, the young person should be encouraged to take the leading role in designing the experiment. Where this is not possible, for example, if the therapist suggests an in-session experiment, the young person must have clear permission to say no. To encourage young people to get involved in the design of experiments, again it will be necessary to be creative and have fun. For example, when carrying out experiments to find out whether thinking something can make it happen, the therapist could encourage the young person to begin by thinking something funny rather than anxiety provoking to see if it comes true, e.g. the therapist's hair turning blue. Once they are comfortable with this, they could then be encouraged to begin to think thoughts that are more anxiety provoking and more related to OCD to see if they work in the same way.

> - Behavioural experiments are an essential component of CBT for young people with OCD.
> - The purpose of experiments is the test the validity of the young person's existing beliefs and to construct and test out new alternative beliefs.
> - Behavioural experiments need to have a clear rationale and, where possible, the young person should be encouraged to take the leading role in designing them.

Relapse prevention

Many young people report that their symptoms increase in times of stress or illness and so it is possible that events such as coming up to exams, moving house or school or changes to friendship groups can reactivate symptoms. As a result, towards the end of treatment it is helpful to introduce this so that the young person is prepared and able to deal with it. Most relapse plans incorporate a review of what was helpful in treatment, consideration of what events could trigger further symptoms, further goals to work towards and then a plan for dealing with setbacks. It can also be helpful to teach the young person to deal with stress and other life difficulties. Towards the end of treatment, increasing the length of time between sessions and offering booster or follow-up sessions can also be helpful.

> A relapse plan involves a review of what was helpful in treatment, consideration of what events could trigger further symptoms, further goals to work towards and a plan for dealing with setbacks.

The therapist's role

The therapist's role is that of an *active listener* who frequently summarises the material they have heard to check their understanding, and is able to respond to different situations in a flexible way. Together the therapist and young person create a formulation of how the current problems are being maintained; for example, how coping behaviours are inadvertently reinforcing thoughts and their meaning. Throughout therapy the therapist acts as a *guide* to help the young person investigate and discover new ways of thinking and behaving. Crucially, the therapist asks questions to identify thoughts and assumptions in order to open up new possibilities, rather than giving concrete advice. In CBT it is not all talk, however; experiencing is also an essential part of learning new ways of thinking and acting. The therapist prompts the young person to devise experiments to test out assumptions where the existing evidence is unclear or unconvincing.

Taking a *non-expert position* also allows the therapist to act as a model for the young person. For example, if the therapist and young person have worked out that the way to find out if touching the toilet bowl will cause a fatal disease is to go ahead and touch it, then the therapist should be prepared to do this first, both to encourage the young person to do the same and as an initial test of the hypothesis. From the therapist's point of view, taking on this role gives greater insight into the discomfort that the young person is likely to be experiencing and a clear realisation of what the young person is being encouraged to do. Recognising the discomfort that will result from behavioural experiments promotes therapist empathy and compassion, both of which are essential to the therapeutic alliance. It might come as a relief to many of us that modelling fallibility can also be extremely useful for clients who set themselves high standards for success. Equally, the non-expert position leaves the therapist free to use personal examples where this is appropriate and there is a clear rationale, for example, normalising intrusive thoughts.

- The therapist is an active listener who acts as a guide to help the young person investigate and discover new ways of thinking.
- It is crucial that they do not take on the role of 'expert' but develop a collaborative relationship with the young person to work together as a team.

The parents' role

Exactly how the young person's family, particularly the parent(s), should be most effectively involved in CBT for OCD has not been clearly defined or evaluated. For example, where family-based CBT has been delivered (e.g. Barrett *et al.*, 2004) it has been compared in different formats (group versus individual family members) rather than compared to non-family-based treatments. Certainly in relation to treatment of other anxiety disorders, outcomes of studies which compare individual child treatment to family treatment have been mixed and it is difficult to draw clear-cut conclusions (Creswell and Cartwright-Hatton, 2007). In the absence of studies to guide us, how we work with families must be determined on an individual basis, through formulation of what is serving to maintain the symptoms. For younger children (pre-adolescents), parents are likely to have a greater influence on their child's developing cognitions (in contrast to adolescents who may be particularly influenced by their peers) (e.g. Rosenberg, 1979), so greater involvement of parents with younger children may give better results (e.g. Barrett *et al.*, 1996a; although see Bodden *et al.*, in press).

CBT with young people across different disorders has involved parents in a number of different ways:

1   *As facilitators*, in which the parent acts as a coach, helping the young person with homework and maintaining the principles of therapy at home.
2   *As co-therapists*, in which the parent models adaptive coping with the therapist and takes on the therapist's role out of sessions; for example, helping the young person to identify thoughts and their meanings, to design experiments and evaluate results.
3   *As clients*, directly targeting parental behaviours which may be accommodating or maintaining OCD such as performing compulsions for the young person, providing excessive reassurance and helping parents to promote the young person's autonomy.

Within each role, parents play an essential part in normalising the young person's experience in order to challenge their fears about what it means to have these thoughts. For this reason, it is essential that parents also receive psychoeducation. Parents need to be able to be open, non-judgemental and not scared of their child's thoughts, moods and behaviours. This is likely to require investigation with the parents of what their child's OCD symptoms mean to them and what they would expect their child to feel or act if put in an anxiety-provoking situation (for example 'My child will not be able to cope' or 'They will go mad'). Perhaps most importantly, the therapist may need to help the parent (by modelling, using Socratic questioning or behavioural experiments) to relax and have fun with their child in order to be confident in their parenting.

Whether and how to include a parent in an individual session will depend on what the goals are of that session, whether the parent(s) have a maintaining role in what is being addressed and how the young person feels about parental participation. As mentioned above, the parent must be included in psychoeducation. They must also have the opportunity to understand the formulation, which may well contrast to the seemingly illogical nature of OCD. If the young person is keen to have sessions independently then this could be done through parallel sessions with the parents, telephone contact or allowing parents to watch videos of the sessions or read the handouts from the sessions. Obviously this needs to be negotiated with the young person and their family.

> Research is limited on how family involvement affects treatment outcome for OCD but some level of family involvement is likely to be essential in order for parents to, at least, have a better understanding of the problem and support treatment.

Involving others

Similarly the involvement of other people, including school personnel, peers and siblings, will be determined by the individual case formulation. For example, if a young person has worries about school germs and a belief that they will become ill if they come into contact with school, it can be helpful to have sessions in school to carry out behavioural experiments. In these cases, this will need to be planned and discussed with the young person's teacher or another appropriate person at school, with the consent of the young person. The young person may also benefit from involving others in behavioural experiments. For example, if they are carrying out compulsions to try to keep their friends safe from harm, they could survey their friends on how they would feel if they were to stop doing the compulsions. Would this make them a bad person or change the way they felt about them as a friend?

- The involvement of others, such as friends or school, can be beneficial, particularly in carrying out behavioural experiments.
- However, this will be determined by the individual case formulation and be based on a clear rationale with the agreement of the young person.

3

Cognitive behavioural assessment of OCD in children and adolescents

Catherine Gallop

Comprehensive assessment of any presenting problem is essential for effective treatment planning and should consist of a detailed and individualised process that is theoretically driven and combines standardised and idiographic measures with clinical interviews. This process is core to the cognitive behavioural assessment of OCD in children and adolescents in the main part due to the diverse content of obsessions and compulsions that are reported. Furthermore, as with any other childhood presenting problem, it is vital that an individualised psychosocial assessment is undertaken to confirm the diagnosis of OCD and so that the young person's OCD can be formulated and treated within their unique context and wider system. The overall aims of cognitive behavioural assessment are as follows:

- to gather detailed information on the young person's main presenting difficulties
- to work towards developing a psychological formulation based on predisposing, precipitating and maintaining factors
- to assess suitability for CBT
- to generate goals for treatment.

In order for these aims to be achieved the therapist should gather information on the following areas:

- family history
- developmental history
- specific OCD symptomatology
- history of OCD
- avoidance and interference
- cognitive appraisals and beliefs
- co-morbidity and risk
- motivation and suitability for treatment.

The therapist should aim to gather information from the young person, their parents (or main carers) and from the young person's wider system (e.g. school) where appropriate (Rapoport and Inoff-Germain, 2000). A clinical interview with the young person with their parents present is recommended in order for a full developmental, family and symptom-based assessment to occur. However, the therapist should be aware that discrepancies between child and parent report can occur. As a general rule priority should be given to the young person's report for internal states (e.g. thoughts and feelings) and to the parents' report for more observable, external behaviours if discrepancies occur. However, parents of adolescents are sometimes unaware of the full extent of their child's symptoms and can therefore underestimate their frequency and severity. In such cases it may be advisable to give greater weight to the report of the young person.

Setting the scene

In addition to the aims of assessment previously highlighted, the assessment process also begins the process of engagement with the young person and their family. For this reason it is often helpful to start the interview by taking a family and developmental history, before moving on to the presenting difficulties. At the beginning of the interview the therapist should explain the areas that will be covered in the assessment and start to build on the idea that assessment (and treatment) is a collaborative process:

> 'I am going to be asking you lots of different questions about your family, about you when you were little and growing up and then about the things that you may be finding difficult at the moment and when they started. There will also be some questionnaires for you and your parents to fill out. You might be thinking that it sounds like an awful lot of questions and you'd be right. The reason there's so many questions is because I want to find out as much about you and your family as possible so that between us we can try and come to the best understanding we can about what's been going on for you and why. This will help us decide what is going to be most helpful in terms of the way forward.'

It is important at this stage to inform the young person and their family that there are no right or wrong answers and that assessment is an ongoing process. Before beginning the assessment, the therapist should discuss and agree with the family whether it would be helpful to have some time as a family together but also to have some time with the young person and family members separately. This can be especially important with adolescents as they often find it difficult to articulate specific thoughts and feelings in front of the parents, such as those of a sexual nature. In addition, it is helpful to spend some time alone with parents to try and elicit parental beliefs and behaviours that may be involved in the maintenance of their child's OCD and that can be hard to discuss in front of their child.

> - The overall aims of cognitive behavioural assessment are to gain information on the young person's main presenting difficulties, to assess suitability for CBT, to develop a psychological formulation, and to generate goals for treatment.
> - Assessment should utilise a range of different measures including structured diagnostic interviews, clinician-rated interviews, self-report questionnaire measures and idiosyncratic measures such as diaries. Information should be gathered from multiple sources and at the very least be based on both child and parent report.

Family and developmental history

The main purpose of taking the family and developmental history is to identify possible vulnerability, precipitating and maintaining factors that can aid formulation and treatment planning. There is clear evidence for the family aggregation of OCD and other anxiety disorders and earlier age of onset has been associated with the presence of OCD in the family (Shafran, 2001). The therapist should therefore enquire about the presence of OCD (both current and past) or other anxiety disorders within the child's family. Given that vulnerability may not only lie in genetic heritability but also socialisation to relevant beliefs and behaviours, specific questioning around the young person's knowledge and experience of the family member's OCD and the way in which the parents feel this may have impacted on the young person may be helpful.

Central to the cognitive behavioural theory of OCD is the notion that normal intrusive thoughts are misinterpreted as being more significant than they really are. It is suggested that certain individuals may be more vulnerable to making these catastrophic misinterpretations (Rachman and Hodgson, 1980) and this may include young people who are prone to anxiety, excessive conscientiousness, perfectionism or depression. The therapist should therefore enquire about early personality characteristics such as the young person's typical reaction to new and potentially anxiety-provoking situations and should note any history of depression or other anxiety disorders. Early obsessional behaviour (and the family member's beliefs and reactions to this) may also be significant in the development of childhood OCD. The therapist should therefore aim to gather detailed information on early obsessive compulsive behaviours and fears but should remain mindful of the distinction between these and normal fears (see Carr, 1999) and behaviours.

Mild obsessions and rituals occur as normal developmental phenomena in children (Evans *et al.*, 1997) and differ from obsessive compulsive symptoms in several ways. Most normal rituals and fears do not usually cause distress or interfere with the child's day-to-day functioning. Normal fears and rituals also occur at specific stages and are then outgrown whereas OCD rituals and worries persist and are developmentally inappropriate. Developmentally appropriate fears tend to be about normal day-to-day themes, whereas although obsessions can be about normal topics, they are often unrealistic or disproportionate to the actual threat. It is therefore helpful for the therapist not only to bear in mind these distinctions when assessing for the presence of both early and current obsessions and compulsions, but also to ask the young person if they feel this is a 'normal worry/behaviour or an OCD one' as most are able to make this distinction.

It is hypothesised that certain beliefs (e.g. about inflated responsibility, thought and action and cognitive control etc.) emerge from early childhood experience and that these beliefs may be associated with the development of OCD (Rachman and Hodgson, 1980; Salkovskis *et al.*, 1999). The therapist should therefore find out about any experiences where the child:

- is given too much responsibility
- is exposed to rigid or extreme codes of conduct or duty
- is left feeling incompetent after being shielded from taking responsibility
- is left feeling actively or passively responsible for significant events or misfortune
- learned that they should be moral in all thought and actions
- learned that they should always have control over their thoughts
- learned that thinking something is equivalent to taking action.

Significant precipitating incidents such as discrete life events or ongoing stressful situations or transitions within the family, at school or involving the media should also be noted, given that a significant proportion of children with OCD develop symptoms following such incidents (Rettew *et al.*, 1992).

Once possible vulnerability and precipitating factors have been explored, the therapist should explore potential family maintaining factors. Various parental responses can have an impact on the continuation of obsessive compulsive symptoms. For example, parents who understandably become involved in their child's rituals as a way of 'helping them get them done more quickly', or who give regular reassurance 'to try and make them realise there is nothing to worry about', or who try to clear their child's path of potential triggers are all inadvertently keeping the problem going. Such responses fail to provide the young person with experiences that allow them to see that their problem is just worry (rather than real danger) and that their obsessions are just normal, insignificant intrusive thoughts (or urges, doubt and images) that they need do nothing about. Furthermore, these responses do not reinforce the young person's own ability to cope with anxiety-provoking situations.

The therapist should also enquire about any parental beliefs relating to the nature and course of their child's OCD; for example, whether they think their child is 'going crazy' or 'just being manipulative and using their OCD to get away with things'. Parents sometimes get into the trap of viewing the OCD as an essential rather than accidental feature of their child, which can have implications on their beliefs about the possibility of change. Whilst enquiring about parental beliefs and behaviours the therapist should consider that the parent's own OCD or anxiety difficulties (if previously identified) may be validating their child's symptoms through modelling. It is also important that the therapist undertakes sensitive enquiry about possible parental maintaining factors and normalises any beliefs or behaviours that are identified.

'We often find that parents start to think and do all sorts of things that they are not sure are actually that helpful because living with a child with OCD is just so difficult. Some parents get involved in their child's rituals or feel that they have to reassure them all the time because it is so hard watching their child suffer at the hands of OCD. Others get really frustrated and annoyed or feel that their child is using their OCD as an excuse for getting out of doing things. Others have given up believing that their child will ever get better because OCD has been around for so long. Do you ever find that you are thinking or doing things that you are not sure are actually helping the problem?'

> The therapist should give special consideration to possible family and environmental factors that may be related to the onset and maintenance of the OCD.

Specific OCD symptomatology

Once potential family and developmental factors have been identified, assessment should focus on gaining information on the young person's primary presenting difficulties. Diagnostic, symptom-based and diary measures are all essential but further idiosyncratic information should be gained via clinical interview. It is important to begin this part of the interview with open questions in order to gain a general description of the nature of the young person's problem: for example, 'Can you tell me about some of the difficulties you have been having recently?' If the young person begins to divulge information that is not relevant to their OCD, it can be helpful to ask them to focus on a recent specific time when their OCD became problematic: for example, 'I am particularly interested in any upsetting thoughts or pictures which have been going through your mind and anything you have had to do because of these thoughts and pictures. Can you tell me about a recent time when you were really bothered by one of these thoughts?'

Once the young person identifies a recent time when they have been bothered by their OCD the therapist should undertake a detailed analysis of any triggering stimuli (which can be internal) or situations; the precise form (i.e. thoughts, picture, urge, doubt) and content (e.g. contamination, harm, symmetry and order, etc.) of the obsessions and the precise nature of any covert (e.g. mental rituals) and overt (e.g. hand-washing, ordering, etc.) neutralising strategies. When asking about the young person's compulsive behaviours it is important to ask about the precise way in which any compulsions brought about relief. The therapist should also enquire about the young person's emotional reaction to the obsessions and any other cognitive or behavioural efforts (e.g. avoidance, looking out for danger, reassurance seeking, arguing back at the thought or trying to block the thought from their mind) that are made in an attempt to control the obsession and its associated distress.

After exploring the recent specific example the therapist should conduct a detailed investigation of all other obsessions and compulsions by asking the young person if they are bothered by any other thoughts or things that they have to do. It can be helpful to give the young person examples of other obsessions and compulsions that are commonly seen and then to ask them if any of the examples are relevant to them. It is also helpful to identify the young person's primary obsessions and compulsions by enquiring about frequency, duration and associated distress. When asking about the levels of distress, it is important to ask not only about distress associated with carrying out compulsions but also any distress experienced by the young person if they are prevented from completing their rituals. Levels of interference and any additional factors that lessen or worsen symptoms should also be noted.

Once the young person's current obsessive compulsive symptoms have been explored, the therapist should ask about the history of the young person's OCD. It is useful to enquire about the initial onset of their symptoms and any potential personal triggering events that have not already been covered in the family interview. Childhood OCD tends to fluctuate over time and it is therefore important to enquire about times when the young person's symptoms have waxed and waned and any ideas they have about why these changes occurred. It is also important to note any changes in the form and content of their obsessions or compulsions given the 'contagious' nature of OCD.

> The young person's current obsessive compulsive symptoms should be identified by reviewing a recent occurrence of their OCD and then via the detailed investigation of possible obsessions and compulsions.

Cognitive appraisals and underlying beliefs

The cognitive behavioural theory views OCD as resulting from assumptions or beliefs that give rise to cognitive biases and faulty appraisals. Given that most adults experience intrusive thoughts similar in content to those reported by individuals with OCD (Salkovskis and Harrison, 1984), it is hypothesised that it is the appraisal (i.e. the expectation, interpretation or evaluation) of intrusive thoughts rather than the thoughts themselves that is problematic and implicit in the development and maintenance of OCD (Salkovskis *et al.*, 2000). There is preliminary support for a downward extension of the beliefs and cognitive appraisals held in adult models of OCD to children (e.g. Barrett and Healy, 2003; Libby *et al.*, 2004).

When conducting the assessment, the therapist should therefore enquire about relevant beliefs and appraisals associated with the young person's obsessions and compulsions. Detailed questioning around the young person's interpretations of their obsessions and compulsions is required by focusing on a recent specific example of when their OCD bothered them. Once the young person has been able to identify their intrusion, the therapist should ask what interpretation they made, for example, 'After you had that thought, what did it mean to you? What was the worst thing that could have happened and why would that have been so awful?' It can be helpful at this stage to offer examples or common misinterpretations:

> 'Sometimes young people think that because they have had this thought, then it will come true. Others think that unless they do something to prevent it something really awful will happen and it will be their fault. Others still think that unless they do something to make themselves feel better they will lose control or go crazy and that the fact that they've had this thought means something bad about them. When you had your thought did it make you think any of these things?'

Information about the young person's beliefs can be obtained via general questioning around how they tend to act or feel in day-to-day situations. Figure 3.1 contains potential questions to guide the therapist when assessing for OCD-related beliefs.

> The therapist should try to identify relevant beliefs and appraisals by asking the young person about their interpretations of their obsessions and compulsions and by examining how they tend to act or feel in day-to-day situations.

Assessing co-morbidity

Given the highly co-morbid nature of OCD, the therapist should be mindful of ascertaining whether OCD is the primary diagnosis and also of making accurate differential diagnosis. Structured diagnostic interviews can be extremely useful in guiding the therapist in making decisions about whether the diagnostic criteria of certain disorders are met. They can also help with

---

Inflated responsibility

> Does the young person believe they have power that is central in causing or preventing negative events?
> Do they believe that if they have any influence over an outcome then they will be ultimately responsible for that outcome?
> Do they believe that not doing something to prevent harm is the same as actually actively causing harm?
> Do they believe that they should try and take any possible action in order to reduce the likelihood of harm happening to others?

Overimportance of thoughts

> Does the young person believe that if they have a thought then it must be important?
> Do they believe it is unacceptable to have intrusions that don't fit with who they are and what they believe?
> Do they believe that their intrusive thoughts are a sign of something meaningful (and negative) about their character?

Overestimation of threat

> Does the young person overestimate the likelihood and severity of possible harm?

Importance of controlling thoughts

> Does the young person believe that they can and should have complete control over their thoughts and mental phenomena?

Intolerance of uncertainty

> Does the young person like to always be certain and find it difficult to cope with change or ambiguous situations?

Perfectionism

> Does the young person believe that they can and should always do something perfectly otherwise they might face serious negative consequences?

Thought–action fusion

> Does the young person believe that having morally unacceptable intrusive thoughts will automatically lead to immoral action and that having a thought is therefore as bad or equivalent to taking action?

Figure 3.1 Assessing for OCD-related beliefs

the issue of identifying what constitutes the primary disorder as they ask for both child and parental report on levels of interference and date of onset of individual disorders. However, due to the significant overlap between symptoms of OCD and other psychological disorders, childhood OCD can be difficult to diagnose and differential diagnosis can be challenging (Merlo _et al._, 2005). When assessing for co-morbidity the therapist should endeavour to distinguish obsessive compulsive symptoms from other clinical phenomena by considering both the common and distinct features of each disorder. Important commonalities and distinctions are highlighted below.

Separation anxiety disorder (SAD) and OCD share the common fear that harm may come to others and both may involve the young person seeking reassurance from parents and family members. However, what distinguishes SAD is that anxiety is limited only to separation from loved ones and no compulsions are undertaken to prevent harm. With generalised anxiety disorder (GAD) the themes are usually about everyday concerns (e.g. school and friendships and family members' health) and are therefore distinguishable from OCD fears, which tend to be more unusual or 'magical' in nature. OCD fears can also be distinguished from the fears in social phobia and with specific phobias where they are limited to social evaluation/ situations and specific objects and situations respectively. Young people with OCD may suffer from panic symptoms due to the intense fear associated with the misinterpretation of their obsessions. However, in order for panic disorder to be diagnosed the young person has to experience repeated, unexpected panic attacks and have persistent anxiety about further impending attacks.

Approximately 30 per cent of young people with OCD also have Tourette's syndrome (TS), where the young person experiences multiple motor or vocal tics (Wagner, 2006). Tics can be defined as sudden, rapid involuntary movements or sounds that occur randomly in a wide variety of situations and are not performed to reduce anxiety or neutralise obsessions. In contrast, compulsions are purposeful, deliberate actions that are performed to reduce anxiety or prevent some undesired outcome. Despite these clear differences, TS and OCD can be difficult to distinguish as some young people with TS report a sense of compulsion with regard to their tics and compulsions are sometimes viewed as sudden and uncontrollable in OCD. Advice from specialists should be sought if difficulties with differential diagnosis of TS and OCD occur and if queries about the impact of TS on the treatment of OCD arise.

Autism and Asperger's syndrome (AS) share clear similarities to obsessive compulsive symptomatology. Young people with autism and AS often have obsessive interests and display stereotypical behaviour, but on the whole these are not associated with anxiety or the prevention of harm. Autism and AS are also manifested by the development of restricted, repetitive patterns of behaviour and interests and sustained impairment in social interactions, whereas young people with OCD tend to display normal social development. Despite these differences, it is of course possible for a young person with AS also to have a diagnosis of OCD and prevalence rates for this dual diagnosis have been estimated at 2 per cent (Lehmkuhl *et al.*, 2007). Although there is extensive research demonstrating the effectiveness of cognitive behavioural interventions for young people with OCD, little is known about how effective these treatments are for children who have a dual diagnosis of OCD and ASD. However, several recent single case studies have shown promising results for the effective use of CBT with young people who have this dual diagnosis (e.g. Lehmkuhl *et al.*, 2007; Reaven and Hepburn, 2003). Furthermore there is increasing evidence that young people with ASD who have anxiety disorders can benefit from both individual and family-based CBT with appropriate developmental adaptations (Chalfant *et al.*, 2007; Sofronoff *et al.*, 2005; Sze and Wood, 2007). If the assessment highlights the presence of both AS and OCD, the therapist should consider the young person's suitability for CBT and seek to adapt the intervention appropriately in line with current findings. Specific guidance may be required from professionals working with this population.

Although differential diagnosis of depression and OCD is not normally problematic, it can be difficult to ascertain which constitutes the primary disorder. In many cases depression is secondary to OCD, although it may warrant being the initial focus of intervention if it is likely to limit the young person's ability to actively engage in treatment for their OCD. The therapist should therefore note that depressive symptomatology can have implications for the successful treatment of OCD and should be reviewed regularly with the young person so that treatment can be adapted appropriately if necessary. If depression is identified the therapist should complete a full risk assessment which should include assessing for the presence and level of self-harming behaviours and suicidal ideation and behaviours (NICE, 2005) and monitor appropriately.

> Due to high levels of co-morbidity in childhood OCD, the therapist should use diagnostic interviews and questionnaire-based measures to try to identify whether OCD is the primary diagnosis and in order to make accurate differential diagnosis.

Assessing motivation and suitability for CBT

CBT is a collaborative treatment that involves the young person taking an active part in sessions and also completing tasks between sessions in the form of monitoring and behavioural experiments. For this reason it is important that the therapist is explicit about the nature of CBT early on in the assessment process and they should ask whether or not the young person feels that it is the right time for them to enter into treatment, for example:

> 'Sessions will involve you and me sitting down together and trying to work out what is going on with your OCD. In particular, we will look at what might be behind the problem getting so upsetting and why the problem has been around for so long. Once we have tried to understand it a little bit more, you will start to try out new ways of dealing with the

problem between sessions and come back and let me know how they have gone. How do you feel about trying to work on your OCD in this way? Does it feel like this is the right time for you to start trying to make things better? Can you see any problems with us working on your OCD in this way right now?'

If the young person has had any previous treatment for their OCD or other difficulties it is important to ask about how they found this experience and to explore whether their previous treatment has any implications for the way you work with them. It can also be helpful at this point to review the pros and cons of staying the same versus changing if motivation appears problematic. If this 'cost-benefit analysis' is undertaken, the therapist should be mindful of exploring and acknowledging their reasons for staying the same before moving on to the pros of change which inevitably involves challenging the continuation of their obsessive compulsive symptoms.

Another issue that is central to the suitability of CBT is the young person's ability to engage in the cognitive components of treatment. This necessarily involves the ability to distinguish thoughts, feelings and behaviours and to identify and evaluate thoughts and cognitive processes (Greenberger and Padesky, 1995). Research from developmental psychology suggests that children from the age of six years can engage in metacognition (i.e. thinking about thinking), recognise inner speech and link thoughts to feelings (Quakley *et al.*, 2003). However, if the therapist has concerns about the young person's ability to engage in these cognitive aspects of CBT it may warrant further assessment. This could involve asking the young person directly if they can tell you how they would describe what thoughts and feelings are and how they relate to each other. Alternatively, the therapist could present the young person with a list of thoughts, feelings and behaviours and ask them to sort them into these categories. Presenting the young person with both ambiguous and potentially anxiety-provoking situations and asking them to identify possible thoughts and the impact of these thoughts (and their interpretations) on feelings and behaviour can also be helpful. If difficulties with the cognitive aspects of CBT or motivation are identified, this does not necessarily preclude the young person from entering into treatment. Preliminary work on motivational issues and understanding thoughts and feelings can be beneficial.

> Motivation and suitability for CBT should be assessed. The pros and cons of change and the young person's ability to engage in the cognitive aspects of treatment should also be considered.

Assessment tools

Diagnostic interviews

Diagnostic interviews have been found to increase the reliability and validity of symptom assessment and diagnosis and aid differential diagnosis (Merlo *et al.*, 2005). Consequently, a diagnostic interview is useful in establishing the diagnosis of OCD, clarifying other diagnoses and deciding which of these is the primary problem for the young person and needs treating first. Therefore, although the use of structured diagnostic interviews for the assessment of OCD and other disorders is most common in research studies, where possible therapists should utilise them in general clinical practice. However, it is worth noting that they can be time-consuming to administer and it may therefore be appropriate to screen for OCD first before administering whole diagnostic interviews. Careful consideration needs to be given to the integration of child and parent report. Greatest reliability will be achieved by combining parent/child data and it is generally regarded as appropriate to favour parent report on observable behaviour and child report for internal subjective experiences (Herjanic and Reich, 1982) if discrepancies occur. Clinicians will require training in the administration of diagnostic interviews. Commonly used diagnostic interviews are outlined below.

The Anxiety Disorders Interview Schedule (ADIS; Silverman and Albano, 1996) is a clinician-administered structured interview, based on *DSM-IV* (APA, 1994) diagnostic criteria and developed specifically for anxiety disorders and their associated conditions. The interview takes approximately an hour and a half to administer with parents and children being interviewed separately. Each section of the ADIS corresponds to a different disorder and complete sections are only administered if initial criteria are reported. A diagnosis is given if appropriate symptoms are present and cause significant interference/clinical distress as indicated by a clinical interference rating of 4 or more (based on a scale of 0 to 8). The clinician then gives the diagnosis a clinical severity rating (0 to 8 point scale) based on the number of symptoms endorsed and the level of interference indicated by the parents and the child. The ADIS has been found to have sound inter-rater and test-retest reliability (Silverman and Albano, 1996).

The Schedule for Affective Disorders and Schizophrenia for School-Age Children (K-SADS-PL; Kaufman *et al.*, 1997) is a clinician-administered diagnostic interview based on *DSM-IV* criteria and adapted from the K-SADS-Present Episode Version (Chambers *et al.*, 1985). Children and parents are interviewed separately and diagnoses are given using clinical judgement and the amalgamation of both reports. The K-SADS-PL begins with an introductory interview that aims to build rapport and acts as the basis for further questioning. Full sections are only completed after initial screening for each disorder is completed. Unlike the ADIS, the K-SADS-PL contains full diagnostic sections on affective, psychotic, substance and eating disorders. Symptoms and impairment are rated on a four-point scale and diagnoses are scored as 'Definite', 'Probable' or 'Not present'. The interview takes approximately 75 minutes to complete. The K-SADS-PL has been found to have good inter-rater and test-retest reliability and sound concurrent validity has also been demonstrated for several diagnoses (Kaufman *et al.*, 1997).

> Structured diagnostic interviews can be used to confirm diagnosis and identify co-morbid conditions.

Clinician-administered measures

Once a diagnosis of OCD has been established, clinician-rated semi-structured interviews can be a helpful way of gaining further information. They allow the clinician to rate the severity of reported OCD symptoms and levels of distress/interference based on clinical judgement and experience as well as concrete prompts.

The Children's Yale-Brown Obsessive Compulsive Scale (CY-BOCS; Scahill *et al.*, 1997) is the most widely used clinician-administered interview for paediatric OCD. This semi-structured interview is adapted from the adult measure (Y-BOCS; Goodman *et al.*, 1989) and is conducted with parents and the young person simultaneously or separately, taking approximately 30 minutes to complete. It asks about the presence of obsessions and compulsion separately over the previous week. Ratings are then given with regard to time occupied, distress and interference caused and levels of control and resistance, using a five-point Likert scale. The overall score (range is between 0 and 40) combines the obsession and compulsion severity sub-scales and gives an overall severity of OCD ranging from mild to extreme. The CY-BOCS has been found to have excellent reliability for obsessions, adequate reliability for compulsions and sound convergent and divergent validity (Scahill *et al.*, 1997). However, the use of the CY-BOCS total score is not strongly supported for clinical or research purposes when it could underestimate symptom severity in a primarily obsessive or primarily compulsive young person (Merlo *et al.*, 2005).

The Leyton Obsessional Inventory – Child Version (LOI-CV) is a 44-item card-sorting task based on the original *Leyton Obsessional Inventory* (LOI-CV; Berg *et al.*, 1988) which contains questions on persistent thoughts, checking, fear of dirt and/or dangerous items, cleanliness, order, repetition and indecision. The LOI-CV yields three distinct scores: 'yes' score (number of questions answered in the affirmative) and 'resistance' and 'interference' scores (where items rated as 'yes' are ranked for levels of resistance and interference in daily life). The LOI-CV has been found to have excellent test-retest reliability and concurrent validity has also been demonstrated (Berg *et al.*, 1988).

The Development and Well-Being Assessment (DAWBA; Goodman

et al., 2000) is a well-validated measure developed for the Survey of British Child Mental Health. It consists of a package of questionnaires, interviews and rating techniques designed to generate *ICD-10* and *DSM-IV* psychiatric diagnoses on young people aged 5 to 16 years old. The structured interviews are administered to both the young person (for 11- to 16-year-olds) and to parents separately. Once definite symptoms have been identified, open-ended questions and prompts are used to get parents and the young person to describe the problem in their own words. Information is brought together by a computer program that predicts possible diagnoses that can then be confirmed or disregarded by an experienced clinical rater.

Questionnaire measures

Self-report and parent-report questionnaire measures can be a quick and often less intrusive method for gathering further details on OCD symptomatology and impairment. Furthermore, they can be used throughout treatment to track change and areas still in need of intervention. However, few validated questionnaires for use with children, especially less than ten years of age, exist. Below is a selection of both validated and non-validated (often newer) questionnaire measures that are commonly administered to young people and their parents which assess core symptoms of OCD, OCD-related beliefs and appraisals and impairment of child and family functioning. Other questionnaire measures such as the *Multidimensional Anxiety Scale for Children* (MASC; March, 1997), the *Screen for Child Anxiety Related Emotional Disorders – Revised* (SCARED-R; Muris *et al.*, 1999) and the *Child Depression Inventory* (CDI; Kovacs, 1992) can also be useful when considering co-morbidity and differential diagnosis.

The *Child Obsessive Compulsive Inventory* (Child OCI; Salkovskis and Williams, 2004a; see Appendix A) is an adapted version of the adult *Obsessive Compulsive Inventory* (OCI; Foa *et al.*, 1998). The OCI consists of 42 items relating to seven subscales (washing, checking, doubting, ordering, obsessing, hoarding and mental neutralising). Each item is rated on a five-point (0–4) Likert scale of symptom frequency and associated distress. The total score is the sum of all subscale scores. A cut-off of 60 has been found to be clinically significant. The OCI has satisfactory reliability and validity (Foa *et al.*, 1998). The Child OCI is a self-report child questionnaire that has been adapted by simplifying the language used and reducing sentence length. In addition, the young person is only required to give distress ratings. Initial normative data for the Child OCI suggests a total mean score of 32.44 in a non-clinical sample (Griffen, 2000). The Child OCI is a useful tool in identifying prominent areas of difficulty and for tracking change throughout therapy.

The *Children's Obsessional Compulsive Inventory* (ChOCI; Shafran *et al.*, 2003) was adapted from the adult OCD measure, the *Maudsley Obsessional Compulsive Inventory* (MOCI; Hodgson and Rachman, 1977). The ChOCI consists of 43 items that are given to both the child and parent which assess the presence and impairment caused by common obsessive and compulsive symptoms. Each item is scored on a three-point scale ranging from 1 'not at all' to 3 'a lot'. A total impairment score of 17 indicates clinically significant OCD. The ChOCI has been found to have adequate psychometric properties (Shafran *et al.*, 2003) although significant correlation between child and parent report on obsessive symptomatology was not found, perhaps owing to the internal and thus non-observable nature of obsessions.

The Leyton Obsessional Inventory – Child Version Survey Form (Leyton CV; Berg *et al.*, 1988) was the first self-report questionnaire to be developed for paediatric OCD. Based on the Leyton card-sorting task, it uses 20 items from the original 44 questions. If a 'Yes' rating is given it is ranked for levels of interference on a four-point scale. A 'Yes' score of greater than 15 and an interference score of greater than 25 have been used to indicate clinical levels of OCD. The survey form demonstrated good internal consistency but test-retest reliability ranges from poor to good depending on the child's age. Furthermore, high false-positive rates and poor concordance with clinical interviews have been found (Allsopp and Williams, 1991; Wolff and Wolff, 1991).

The Child Obsessive Compulsive Impact Scale (COIS; Piacentini and Jaffer, 1999) is a 56-item measure assessing the level of impairment caused by OCD on the child's day-to-day functioning over the previous month. Items relate to potential difficulties in school, home and social activities and are rated on a four-point scale ranging from 'not at all' to 'very much'. The COIS has demonstrated good psychometric properties and is sensitive to treatment effects.

The Child Responsibility Interpretation Questionnaire and *Child Responsibility Attitude Scale* (CRIQ and CRAS; Salkovskis and Williams, 2004b; see Appendix B) are two companion child-report measures which have been adapted from the adult *Responsibility Interpretation Questionnaire Scale* and *Responsibility Attitude Scale* (RIQ and RAS; Salkovskis *et al.*, 2000). The CRIQ is a 15-item questionnaire that measures the frequency and strength of belief in appraisals of responsibility associated with intrusive thoughts. The CRAS is a measure of general responsibility attitudes (assumptions) and consists of 20 items that ask the child to rate a series of statements such as 'I often feel responsible for things that go wrong' on a seven-point scale. Initial investigation into these adapted measures has indicated high internal consistency and concurrent validity and initial normative data has suggested overall mean scores of 17.4 (frequency) and 451.7 (belief) on the CRIQ and 64.17 on the CRAS (Griffen, 2000).

The Family Accommodation Scale (FAS; Calvacoressi *et al.*, 1995) is a parent-report measure that assesses family involvement in the maintenance of OCD. It consists of nine items relating to the accommodation of the child's obsessive and compulsive behaviour over the previous month. Each item is rated on a five-point scale. The FAS has demonstrated satisfactory levels of inter-rater reliability. However, more research on its psychometric properties is needed.

> Clinician administered and self-report questionnaires provide a useful way of quantifying symptoms and can be used to monitor change.

Idiosyncratic measures

Idiosyncratic measures such as diaries are helpful in targeting specific obsessive compulsive symptoms, including the daily frequency and distress associated with the young person's primary obsessions and compulsions, details on eliciting stimuli and levels of anxiety experienced. These measures can be a useful way of gaining baseline information but also allow the therapist to track change throughout treatment. This is a vital aspect of treatment, given that factors such as the reduction in young persons' daily experience of obsessions have been found to be a primary indicator of treatment success with adults (Clark, 2004). The use of diaries to identify and challenge the young person's interpretation of intrusive thoughts is also crucial in cognitive behavioural therapy for OCD. Appendix C contains examples of diaries that can be used with young people and their parents.

Specific issues in the assessment of OCD with young people

Clark (2004) notes that obsessive compulsive symptoms and characteristics such as the need for exactness, concern about making mistakes, pathological doubt and indecision can all interfere with the assessment process and make the completion of questionnaires and the clinical interview difficult. Completion of questionnaires and the clinical interview may also elicit obsessions and compulsions which the therapist will have to help the young person manage. It is important that the therapist acknowledges the young person's anxiety and the fact that OCD can make assessment difficult. It is helpful to be clear about the purpose of assessment, to limit the number of measures and to give the young person plenty of time to respond. It can also be useful to develop a joint plan of how to manage the assessment process with minimal distress and to identify and challenge any faulty assumptions the young person may have about what will happen. For example, if the young person is wary of taking part in the assessment process because they are concerned about their resultant levels of anxiety, the therapist could ask them to consider a previous time when they had been in an anxiety-provoking situation and explore previous coping strategies and whether the outcome was as they had predicted.

Another issue relating to the assessment of OCD is the difficulty some young people have in identifying and discussing primary obsessions and interpretations. It has been suggested that up to 40 per cent of young people do not have clear obsessions (Carr, 1999). For others, their compulsive behaviour has become so habitual that they have gone past being able to draw a clear link between an intrusion, their interpretation and their resultant neutralising behaviour. In such cases it is best to proceed with acknowledging an urge to perform their compulsion and a sense that it would feel awful if they did not complete it. The therapist can then return to trying to identify the obsession and its interpretation once the compulsion has been explored by asking the young person 'When you had the urge to do X, what do you think was the worst thing that could happen if you did not put it right?' Alternatively the therapist can ask the young person to let them know the next time they get an urge to complete a compulsion and before they carry it out ask them what is going through their mind and what would be the worst thing about not performing the compulsion.

The issue of shame or embarrassment can also make it difficult for young people to disclose the content of their obsessions and misinterpretations. Some are reluctant because they are fearful of the potential consequences (e.g. 'You might phone the police or have me locked up') or worry what the therapist may think of them (e.g. 'Some of my thoughts are so bad it will make you think that I'm an awful person and you won't want to help me.'). In such situations the therapist should acknowledge the young person's difficulty with discussing their thoughts and should also aim to normalise the content of common intrusive thoughts and fears that many young people have:

> 'I can see that it is really hard for you to talk about your OCD worries. This happens a lot of the time because OCD thoughts tend to be about our worst nightmare; the kinds of things we don't think should go through our heads. But it's actually completely normal to have nasty or scary things come into our heads and what's more we have no control of what comes into our heads. OCD is very clever, as it tends to pick on the people that are sensitive and perhaps even care too much. It likes the fact that you are bothered by the thoughts and it knows they will bother you because they're actually the complete opposite for what you stand for. Would it be helpful if I gave you some examples of the kinds of thoughts that sometimes go through my head and the young people I have seen?'

Due to phenomenological overlap with other disorders, alternative explanations for symptoms need to be excluded and the core features of obsessions and function of compulsions should be explored. Clark (2004) notes the core features of obsessions, which can be useful in distinguishing obsessions from other types of mental phenomena. These include the fact that the obsessions:

- are intrusive (enter the mind against the young person's will)
- cause distress
- are ego-dystonic (inconsistent with the young person's core values)

- are uncontrollable
- are associated with a strong urge to suppress or resist.

Compulsions can be distinguished by the fact that they are purposeful acts that the young person feels driven to perform in response to their obsessions or associated distress.

> - The therapist should be clear about the purpose of assessment and limit the number of measures.
> - Issues such as shame or embarrassment or fearing the consequences of disclosing symptoms can make it difficult for young people to disclose the content of their obsessions and misinterpretations.

4

Planning and carrying out treatment

Polly Waite, Catherine Gallop and Linda J. Atkinson

CBT Model

This treatment approach is based on Salkovskis' (1985) cognitive model of OCD, but modified in order to work with young people and families. This model proposes that in individuals with OCD the normal phenomena of intrusive thoughts are misinterpreted as meaningful and seen as an indication that they might be responsible for harm to themselves or others unless they take preventative action. As a result, the individual attempts to suppress and neutralise the thought through compulsions, avoidance, seeking reassurance or by attempting to get rid of the thought. The aim of these neutralising behaviours is to reduce perceived responsibility. However, they actually make further intrusive thoughts more meaningful and more likely to occur, evoke more discomfort and lead to further neutralising. The key components of therapy are:

- carrying out an individualised formulation
- psychoeducation
- establishing goals
- developing an alternative way of making sense of the problem
- testing this out through behavioural experiments
- relapse prevention.

This approach has similarities with traditional ways of working with young people with OCD (e.g. March and Mulle, 1998) in that it involves techniques such as externalising the OCD in order to separate it from the child and family and the use of metaphors and stories. It also involves a large behavioural component in order to get rid of OCD. In both approaches, treatment is predictable and the young person has explicit control over what they carry out inside and outside sessions. However, there are also key differences:

1   March and Mulle's (1998) treatment package involves extensive discussion of OCD as a medical illness and compares it to illnesses such as diabetes. Our approach is based on the idea that OCD stems from misunderstanding thoughts and that stressing biological factors can be unhelpful, in that it can lead to children and families feeling that there is something wrong with them and that it may not be treatable.

2   March and Mulle's treatment involves a cognitive component, in that youngsters learn cognitive tactics for resisting OCD, such as constructive self-talk ('bossing back the OCD') and positive coping strategies to use during exposure and response prevention (ERP). In contrast, this approach sees faulty cognitions at the heart of the problem and so treatment focuses on psychoeducation about thinking in OCD, works to identify the young person's beliefs and then tests out whether these beliefs are true.

3   This is done through behavioural experiments that are set up in order to find out how the world really works. This differs from traditional approaches where the cornerstone of treatment is ERP, involving a graded hierarchy that the young person works their way through. Within our approach, there is no hierarchy as young people are encouraged to carry out experiments that relate to their specific beliefs and treatment goals. Rather than having a list of tasks that they have to work through, they are encouraged to take a curious stance to try to understand how the problem is working and experiments are devised in order to learn information. Very often the young person will choose to start with tasks that are less anxiety provoking in order to be able to achieve them and leave the most difficult experiments to later sessions. However, this comes from the child, giving them more flexibility and allowing them to feel more in control of the process.

- OCD arises from misunderstanding thoughts.
- Behavioural experiments are designed to test specific predictions.

Number of sessions

Before treatment begins, it is helpful to give the young person and family an idea of the number of sessions that may be required. This can assist the young person to feel that the problem is treatable and that they will not need therapy indefinitely. It can keep momentum going and also supports the idea of the young person taking increasing amounts of responsibility in therapy as they work towards ending treatment. The number of sessions will depend on the severity of the problem as well as any co-morbid problems or other issues that may need to be addressed. Treating the OCD may have a beneficial effect on other problems (especially other anxiety disorders) as the young person learns skills that they can apply elsewhere. However, it may be necessary for treatment also to focus on other problems, such as self-esteem or family factors. While a young person with mild to moderate OCD and little co-morbidity may require as few as five treatment sessions, youngsters with more severe problems are likely to benefit from a greater number and clinicians may need to consider somewhere between 12 and 20 sessions. Although there is a relationship between early response in treatment and success at follow-up (e.g. Allsopp and Verduyn, 1988), there is also evidence to suggest that initial non-responders may show significant improvements when therapy is extended (e.g. de Haan *et al.*, 1998), so clinicians should always ensure that the young person has received an adequate dose of CBT.

Planning treatment

At the end of the initial assessment, the therapist should be clear that the primary problem is OCD and remain aware of any other existing diagnoses and how they interact with the young person's OCD. The therapist will have gained information about other factors that may be relevant in planning treatment, such as how the OCD is managed within the family and the impact on school functioning. By this stage, they will have collected much of the information necessary to begin making sense of the problem, understand why the problem has persisted for so long and why it has been so difficult to get rid of it. Specifically, it is helpful to have an idea about any triggers and precipitating factors that may be maintaining the OCD before treatment begins.

When planning the first session, the therapist needs to think about who should actually be in the room for the session. This decision will be driven by factors such as the initial formulation about how the problem is working and the wishes of the young person. If family members are present, it can be helpful to share the formulation and any psychoeducation about the nature of intrusive thoughts and anxiety. There are good reasons to include family members if the therapist believes that their behaviour may be maintaining the problem, for example, through giving reassurance or undertaking compulsions for the young person. It can also be helpful to have family members present if the assessment has highlighted that the young person tends to minimise the extent of their OCD. However, this must be balanced with the views of the young person and for adolescents especially having family members present may not always be appropriate. For example, the presence of the parent may be a form of reassurance, or the parent may be highly critical or anxious within the session (e.g. speaking on behalf of the young person too much). In other cases, the young person may find it hard to talk openly in front of their parents or they may feel responsible for not worrying their mum or dad with their concerns. In these cases, it may be possible to negotiate other solutions with the young person, such as taping or videoing the session and allowing family members to watch or listen to some or all of them, having them present for certain parts of the session or having some time with the family members alone to go through important issues at the end of the session.

Carrying out CBT

At the beginning of the first session, it is important that the therapist provides information about the nature and process of CBT:

1   The therapist explains that they will all be *working as a team* to try and deal with the problem.
2   In many ways *the young person is the 'expert'* because they are the one who knows how their OCD works on a day-to-day basis. It can be helpful to emphasise that one of their jobs is to teach everyone else about the problem so everyone understands how it currently works.
3   It is helpful if the young person understands that *CBT is an active treatment* where they will have to try out different and new ways of dealing with the problem. This can be achieved by asking the young person what problems they anticipate if the sessions just involved talking about the OCD and not trying out anything new.
4   The importance of *trying out tasks outside the sessions* needs to be highlighted and again it can be helpful to get the young person to think about the purpose of these tasks to build motivation and encourage the young person to 'own' them. Tasks between sessions are not just for the young person and there may be times when it is appropriate for the therapist or family members to try things out to get extra information and model tackling the problem.
5   The therapist should inform the young person that each session will *start by setting an agenda* so that they can plan and prioritise what they are going to talk about during the session. The young person and family members should be encouraged to add items to the agenda and be involved in deciding what the most important things to be covered are.

- When planning the first session, the therapist needs to think about who will be in the room for sessions.
- At the beginning of the first session, the therapist needs to provide information about the nature and process of CBT.
- The young person needs to understand that CBT is an active

treatment that involves trying out different and new ways of dealing with the problem.

- Sessions start by setting an agenda to plan and prioritise what they are going to talk about during the session.

The young person's understanding of OCD

At the beginning of therapy, the therapist will aim to explore the young person's understanding of OCD, and specifically what they think obsessions and compulsions are and how they relate to each other. There may be some words that the young person feels uncomfortable with, for example, some young people prefer not to use the word 'ritual' as for them it conjures up ideas of witchcraft. Consequently, this discussion should also involve finding out what the young person already calls or would prefer to call obsessions (e.g. 'worries' or 'thoughts'), compulsions (e.g. 'habits', 'rituals', 'jobs') and the OCD generally (e.g. 'OCD', 'the worry monster'). This also helps to externalise the OCD and reinforce the idea that it is the OCD that is the problem, not the young person.

Making sense of the problem

Once this is established and the young person can clearly identify the difference between obsessions and compulsions, the focus of the first treatment session is to gain a greater understanding of the problem. The young person and the therapist begin to build a picture of how the problem is working. It can be helpful to begin by asking the young person to think of a recent time where OCD was a problem. They should try to recall a time that is fairly fresh in their memory and that is typical of how the problem often arises. Once they have identified a time, the therapist encourages them to tell them more about the situation in order to prime their memory. This includes when it was, where they were, whether anyone else was present and what happened just before. It is important to remember that the trigger to an episode of OCD can be external (e.g. seeing something on television) or internal (e.g. remembering something bad that has happened in the day). Once this has been established, the therapist moves on to help the young person identify what was going through their mind, what they made of the thought (or picture or urge), how it made them feel and what it made them do. The therapist should frequently summarise what they have learned in order to clarify their understanding and make the young person feel that the problem is understood. As well as asking about compulsions, it is important to prompt for other behaviours that may contribute to the maintenance of the problem, including any avoidance, reassurance seeking, hypervigilance (i.e. being on the alert and looking out for danger), emotional responses, arguing or trying to push the thought out.

Jack was an 11-year-old boy who described a range of obsessions and compulsions which had been around for a few years. One of the most disturbing obsessions for him was the thought or image of harming his younger brother Charlie. Jack and his therapist used this obsession to start to develop an understanding of how the problem was working:

Therapist: So Jack, if I've got this right, you were in the park with your brother Charlie and your dad and it was Sunday afternoon and you had just finished a game of football. You and Charlie decided to climb onto the climbing frame and you were right at the top.

Jack: That's right and I was feeling happy because I had scored a goal.

Therapist: Okay and you were feeling happy because you had just scored a goal. So what was the first sign of trouble?

Jack: I was leaning over the bar at the top of the climbing frame and suddenly imagined Charlie lying under the bar and me squashing him. I started to feel really sad and wanted to go home. I started to cry and Charlie wanted to know why but I couldn't tell him. I told Dad that I wanted to go home.

Therapist: And when you had that picture of squashing Charlie under the climbing frame, what did you believe that meant?

Jack: That the next time Charlie and I might be playing in the park, I might do it, but I wouldn't!

Therapist: Even though you know you wouldn't, you felt worried that the next time you and Charlie were playing in the park you might squash him.

Jack: Yes.

Therapist: And so you felt sad and wanted to go home.

Jack: Yes.

Therapist: Other than sad, did it make you feel anything else?

Jack: I felt guilty, like I'm a bad brother, and I felt hurt.

Therapist: That doesn't sound like a very nice feeling. When you had that picture of squashing Charlie did you do anything to try to make the thought better?

Jack: Yes, I touched the climbing frame and thought that I love Charlie and when I got home I told Mum what I had thought and asked her whether I would really do it and she said not to worry about it.

Therapist: Did you do anything else, like staying away from Charlie or anything you thought could be dangerous?

Jack: Well I didn't really want to play with Charlie later in case I did something and also I made sure that there wasn't anything in the playroom that I could use to squash him.

> *Therapist:* And when you had that thought of squashing Charlie, did you try and push the thought out or argue against it?
>
> *Jack:* I tried to argue with the thought. I tried to say to myself that I would never do it.

At this stage it is often helpful to have a discussion about knowing things in your head and knowing them in your heart. Jack describes how he knows that he would not hurt Charlie but also describes feeling that he might do it. Typically, the person 'knows' that their obsessions may be senseless, but in the situation 'feels' differently. As a result, they may feel embarrassed in the session when they are identifying their intrusive thoughts. At this time, it can be helpful for the therapist to say something like 'I've learned that OCD doesn't work at a brain level and that is not about what you know in your head but what you feel in your heart' and to check out with the young person if they feel that this is the case for them too. Making this differentiation now can be helpful later on in therapy when the therapist is trying to track belief change so that the young person understands that the focus is on what they believe at the time of the obsession rather than later, in the session.

Some young people may be reluctant to recall and discuss anxiety-related cognitions that are related to anticipated danger (Clark and Beck, 1988) and may experience intense emotion as they may fear negative consequences associated with talking about their worries (e.g. that the worry may come true) or that the therapist may think they are bad or crazy. If the young person is hesitant in voicing their obsession, the therapist should gently persist in trying to identify the thought and normalise different kinds of thoughts (including the therapist's own thoughts) to try to make the young person feel more comfortable. It can also be helpful to try and identify and deal with the young person's specific worries relating to talking about their obsessions by asking questions such as 'What upsets you most about talking about these things?' or 'In your worst nightmare what could happen if you talk about these things?' Once the worries have been identified the therapist should help the young person see that their feared predictions are unlikely to come true; for example, by asking them whether something bad has ever happened to them by talking about these things and informing them that it is very rare for 'bad' people to get OCD as 'bad' people aren't normally bothered by nasty thoughts.

By the end of the discussion, the therapist and young person will have drawn out a shared formulation. Younger children can enjoy drawing it out themselves and they should be encouraged to add pictures or symbols to make the diagram more meaningful. Jack's formulation (Figure 4.1) illustrates how the problem is working. An intrusive thought pops into his mind and is interpreted as being meaningful (i.e. it could come true unless he does something to stop it and that it means he is a bad brother). This leads him to feel bad, sad, hurt and guilty and as a consequence he carries out a compulsion (touching the climbing frame and saying 'I love Charlie' in his head) and other safety behaviours (such as asking for reassurance from his mum and arguing with the thought). However, these behaviours lead him to

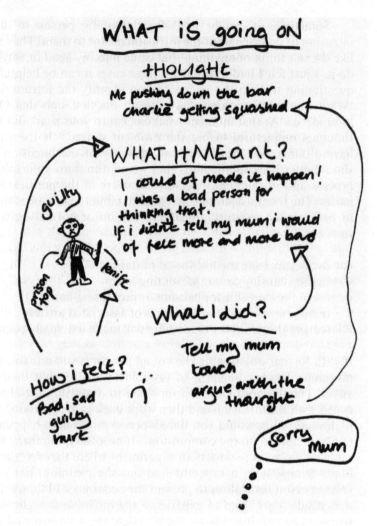

Figure 4.1   Jack's formulation

experience more intrusive thoughts and to believe more strongly that the meaning attached to the thoughts is true, thereby maintaining and exacerbating the problem.

   Once the formulation has been drawn, the therapist should check with the young person that it is an accurate representation of what went on, make necessary amendments and ask the young person to summarise what has been drawn to check their understanding. The therapist should then ask the young person whether they feel this drawing would make sense for other times when their OCD has been a problem. If the young person feels that this is not the case, it can be helpful to repeat the formulation process for a different episode to highlight the fact that, whatever the situation, OCD tends to work in the same way.

Sometimes it can be hard for the young person to identify a clear intrusion or describe what the intrusion meant to them. They may say things like 'I can't think of anything that came into my head or why I felt I should do it, I just felt I had to do it!' In these cases it can be helpful to try further questioning to help the young person identify the intrusion: for example, 'What was the first thing you noticed, the first sign that OCD might be around?' or 'At that moment what came into your head, did you notice any thoughts or pictures before the problem started?' If the young person is having difficulties identifying the meaning of the intrusion, the therapist should refer back to any hints that were given during the initial assessment process and in the young person's answers in the pre-treatment questionnaires. The therapist should also bear in mind the key areas that are thought to be associated with the misinterpretation of normal intrusions in OCD such as:

- over-estimating the likelihood of danger
- fearing causing or not preventing harm
- feeling responsible for causing or preventing harm
- fearing unrealistic consequences of associated anxiety
- fearing that thinking something will make it actually come true.

If with further questioning the young person is still not able to identify the meaning, it can be helpful to proceed by saying that their intrusion felt awful. The therapist can then move on to discussing the compulsion associated with the intrusion and then work backwards by asking 'In your worst nightmare, what would you have worried might have happened if you had not been able to do the compulsion?' If necessary, the therapist should help the young person to design an experiment where they refrain from carrying out a compulsion in order to find out the meaning. For example, if the young person neutralises to prevent the occurrence of thoughts the therapist may need to get them to experience the intrusive thought (image or urge) without neutralising and ask them to describe what happens.

- In the first session, the therapist needs to find out what the young person calls or would prefer to call obsessions, compulsions and OCD generally.
- The focus is then on gaining a greater understanding of the problem and this is done by reviewing a recent occasion where OCD was around.
- The therapist and young person then draw out a formulation which shows how the problem is working and being maintained.

The vicious cycle of OCD

Once the young person feels that the picture of what happened is complete, the next step is to create doubt within the child about the usefulness of their responses. This is achieved by suggesting the possibility that the things they are doing (such as compulsions or avoidance) are actually making the problem worse as they strengthen the meaning they have attached to their intrusion and do not provide them with the opportunities to discover that their feared consequences do not come true. This in turn means they are more likely to keep doing the compulsions and other unhelpful behaviours. Sometimes the young person may have already reached this conclusion whilst trying to make sense of what happened. For example, they may have commented that they try to push the thought out, but this does not work and the thought comes back stronger and this gives the therapist a way in. However, this is not always the case and can be one of the most difficult parts of the session, as very often the young person has not made sense of the problem in this way before and has been seeing the behaviours as the way of getting rid of the thought and making themselves feel better, not worse. Consequently, the therapist should take whatever time is needed to help the young person understand these feedback processes and may need to use a number of different strategies such as guided discovery, psychoeducation, role play, storytelling and metaphors. It can also be helpful to begin the process of explaining feedback loops and vicious cycles by focusing on the most prominent response strategies (e.g. ritual, avoidance or looking for danger) that the young person identified in the formulation, for example, with Jack:

Therapist: Okay Jack, I'm a bit confused and I wonder if you can help me. You've told me all about this problem with getting horrible thoughts and the things OCD gets you to do to make the problem better and get rid of the thoughts. The bit I'm confused about is that you've also told me that over time this problem has got worse and worse rather than getting better. Is that right?

Jack: Yes.

Therapist: So I wonder whether the things OCD has been telling you to do might actually be making the problem worse, even though it tells you that it is going to be making it better. Do you think that could be the case?

Jack: Maybe?

Therapist: I wonder if it's a bit like if a carpenter was using sandpaper on a door that is too big to fit the frame. He keeps using the sandpaper over and over because it seems to be a good idea at first. The problem is he keeps sanding it so much that eventually the door won't fit because it's now too small! His solution actually became the problem!

Jack: I get it, but how is that the same as my OCD?

Therapist: Well let's have a look. Let's see how doing habits might be causing part of the problem. Now if I have got this right, you believed in your heart that unless you touched the climbing frame and thought about how you loved Charlie you might have squashed him. Is that right?

Jack: Yes I know I wouldn't but I was really worried that I might.

Therapist: Now when you did the habit and then you didn't hurt Charlie, what did this make you think?

Jack: I guess that if I hadn't done it I might have actually hurt him.

Therapist: Can you see what the problem with that is? Can you see what you don't get to find out?

Jack: I guess that maybe I wouldn't have done it even if I hadn't done the habit.

Therapist: That's exactly right. I guess you don't know that anything bad would have happened if you hadn't carried out the ritual. You don't know whether your ritual made any difference at all. I'm going to tell you a little story that I think might help us think about your rituals. . . .

Say there was a man standing in [a place near Jack's home] with his pockets full of salt. The man is throwing piles of salt everywhere. People think what he is doing looks very strange. Someone goes up to the man and asks, 'Why are you throwing salt all over the floor?' and the man replies, 'To keep the alligators away!!'

What do you make of this story?

Jack: It's a bit silly. I mean why would he be throwing salt? You don't get alligators where I live.

Therapist: That's what I think too, but how come the man doesn't know that?

Jack: Because he thinks they're not coming because he's throwing the salt.

Therapist: Exactly! What do you think he would have to do to find out what we all know?

Jack: Stop throwing the salt and wait and see if any come. Perhaps he could hide just in case!

Therapist: That sounds like a good idea. How might that story relate to your habits?

Jack: Well I guess I'm like the man throwing the salt, apart from I'm worried about hurting people not alligators!

Therapist: That's right, so if you're similar to the man throwing salt, what do you think you might need to do?

Jack: Stop doing the habits and see what happens?

Therapist: That sounds like a really good idea!

This also illustrates the usefulness of metaphors, stories and imagery to help the young person to make sense of what is going on. Chapter 5 provides more examples of metaphors that can be helpful to use with young people.

- The formulation is used to think about whether compulsions (and other responses, such as avoidance or seeking reassurance) may actually keep the problem going and act as a vicious cycle.

- This can be difficult and so the therapist may need to use a range of different strategies including guided discovery, psychoeducation, role play, storytelling and metaphors.

Psychoeducation

Early on in therapy, the therapist also picks up on some 'basic facts' of OCD that start to help the young person to think differently about their OCD. As discussed in Chapter 1, there is good evidence that most of the population have intrusive thoughts. This information is critical in starting to think about the problem in a different way. It can be helpful to ask the young person and their family to begin by estimating what percentage of the population have intrusive thoughts, pictures or doubts and then let them know that in fact about 90 per cent of the population report having them. The therapist can use this as an opportunity to challenge any beliefs that the young person may have had about themselves (e.g. that they were going mad or are a bad person) and enable them to see that actually these thoughts meant that they were normal. The therapist may also let the young person know that thoughts tend to be about things that are meaningful or important to us. For example, Jack's thought of harming people he loves came along when his younger brother Charlie was born and there was an understandable feeling of sibling rivalry, but at the same time a worry about hurting his new brother given he was so small and vulnerable.

Once the young person accepts that it is normal to have intrusive thoughts, they may still feel that they could solve the problem if they could get control of them or even get rid of them completely. It can be helpful to use a behavioural experiment at this point to demonstrate that it is not possible to control your thoughts. The therapist may have the child and family try not to think of a pink giraffe to demonstrate that when they try not to think about something it inevitably pops into their mind. It can also be helpful to have a discussion about what life would be like if you never had a thought coming into your mind uninvited and that we need thoughts to pop into our heads in order to be creative human beings.

Once the therapist and the young person have established that intrusive thoughts are normal, not bad and something which we can't and shouldn't try to control, the therapist then moves on to thinking with the young person that if the problem is not the intrusive thought, which part of the formulation helps them to understand where the problem lies? As with the vicious cycles, it can help to give real life examples or role play and think about two young people with the same thought (e.g. 'Have I left my hair straighteners plugged in?' or 'Have I left the computer turned on?') that respond to it in a different way (e.g. one thinks 'There could be a fire and our house could burn down and it would be my fault' and so goes back and checks or asks their mum if they have left the plug in, while the other thinks 'That's just a silly thought' and carries on without doing anything). Once the young person reaches the conclusion that it is the meaning of the thought or how the thought is interpreted that is important, it is helpful to think further about how different thoughts mean different things to different people at different times. This is particularly relevant for young people who have thoughts about harming others and have beliefs around them being a bad person.

Therapist:	Jack, I want you imagine that there is a boy sitting in the chair next to you and he is crying because he has just had a picture in his head and the picture is of him being in church and him shouting swear words at God. What kind of boy would find that picture so upsetting?
Jack:	I think he would be religious?
Therapist:	How come?
Jack:	Because he cares about God and that's why he is so bothered.
Therapist:	I see. Yes, that makes sense. So, I'm wondering what your thought means about you?
Jack:	I thought it meant I was a bad brother, but now I think it means I love my brother and that's why it makes me feel like crying when I get the thought.
Therapist:	Okay, so you thought you were a bad brother but now you realise that actually it is the complete opposite. OCD made you think you were a bad brother but we know that really you are a lovely brother and that's why you felt so sad. I think I get it. That's why OCD is so sneaky, it actually picks things that we really care about and tends to pick people who are most bothered by these thoughts. But the good news is it also picks the people who are least likely to do these things because they care so much.

- Psychoeducation enables the young person and their family to think differently about the OCD.
- Most of the population experience the same kinds of intrusive thoughts, urges or images as people with OCD, but it is the meaning they attach to them that is the problem.

> • It is impossible to get rid of intrusive thoughts completely or to be able to control them and so the aim of therapy is to think about them in a different, less threatening way.

Understanding how anxiety works

The therapist should also explore the young person's beliefs about what will happen to their anxiety if they do not perform a compulsion or take other action, such as avoidance. For example, Katie was a 14-year-old girl who had been badly bullied at school. Although the bullying had stopped, she had a great number of obsessional worries, including about being bullied again. As a result, she repeated actions a certain number of times, such as going through doorways a lucky number of times. She believed that by doing this she was making sure that she would not be bullied again. She also believed that if she did not do the compulsions, she would be so worried that she would not be able to deal with it and her anxiety would 'go through the roof'. Figure 4.2 shows the graph that Katie drew to illustrate what OCD had been telling her would happen if she did not do compulsions. The therapist then went on to explain to Katie how anxiety works:

> *Therapist:* Katie, we know a bit about how anxiety or worry works generally and that when we feel worried a chemical called adrenalin pumps through our body and sends lots of energy to our muscles. So if you imagine being an animal in the jungle centuries ago, this helps you to run away if you are in a dangerous situation. But it only works for short periods of

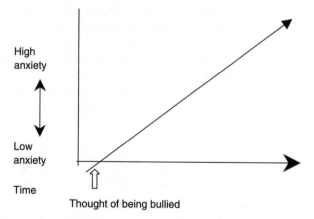

Figure 4.2   Katie's graph showing what OCD predicts will happen to her anxiety if she does not do a compulsion

time to get you out of the situation and then it goes down. Can you draw me a graph like before, but this time, show anxiety going up and then slowly going down in a curve?

Katie then draws another graph (see Figure 4.3).

Therapist: What we also know is that for most people, their anxiety works like this and that includes situations like OCD. What I'm interested to know is whether this could be the same for you? Are there ever times when you have gone against what OCD has told you to do?

Katie: I don't know. I can't think of any times I haven't done what OCD says.

Therapist: Are there any other times when you have felt nervous or worried, like before a test?

Katie: I was nervous before a race on Sport's Day.

Therapist: And what happened to those feelings?

Katie: Once I started running they weren't so bad and after a bit I forgot about it.

Therapist: So which of these two graphs did it look like?

Katie: This one [points to Figure 4.3].

Therapist: What do you think that might mean in OCD situations?

Katie: I suppose it could be the same.

Therapist: Okay, so let's imagine that you go against what the OCD says and you find out that your anxiety goes down. What would you imagine might happen the next time?

Katie: Well, if nothing bad happened, I think it could get easier?

Therapist: How come?

Katie: Well I've done it before, so I know it's going to be okay.

Therapist: And if you did it again?

Katie: I think if I did it enough times and nothing bad happened then I wouldn't be worried any more.

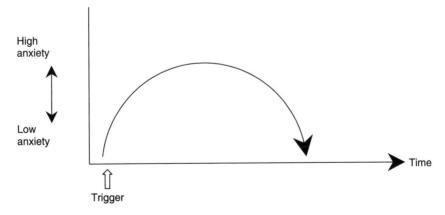

Figure 4.3 Katie's graph showing what normally happens to anxiety

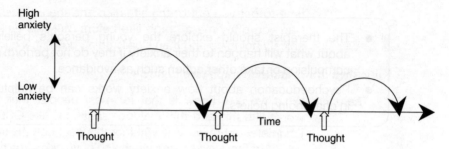

Figure 4.4   Katie's graph showing what could happen to anxiety over time if you do not do a compulsion

Therapist: So can you show me what that would look like with another graph?

Katie draws another graph (see Figure 4.4).

Therapist: So, how do we find out if it works like this for you?
Katie: I could try not to do something four times and just do it normally?
Therapist: And what would you predict would happen?
Katie: OCD would predict it would go through the roof, but I think that it might work like it did when I did on Sport's Day and after a while it might go down.
Therapist: That sounds like a good way to find out.

It can also be useful at this point to have a conversation about what OCD is currently doing to the young person's levels of anxiety. Most young people will soon realise that although doing a compulsion helps in the moment because it reduces their anxiety, it does not help in the longer term as the next time they get an intrusive thought or urge their anxiety goes up just as high and they spend their day-to-day life going up and down the 'anxiety yo-yo' (see Figure 4.5).

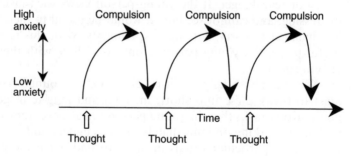

Figure 4.5   What happens to anxiety if you do compulsions

> - The therapist should explore the young person's beliefs about what will happen to their anxiety if they do not perform a compulsion or take other action such as avoidance.
> - Psychoeducation about how anxiety works can be helpful in challenging beliefs.

Goal setting

Within the first two sessions it is important to establish clear, realistic goals for treatment. At times, it can be tempting to overlook the importance of establishing goals, especially if there is time pressure or a desire to begin treatment as soon as possible. Although there may be times when you can get away without establishing clear goals, this can lead to later problems. This is because part-way through treatment the young person will often appear to reach a halt in therapy. Progress is not as fast as could be expected, or perhaps the young person fails to see any personal usefulness in carrying on with treatment. It is important to remember that for many young people the reason they present for treatment is because an adult in their lives, typically one of their parents, has decided for various reasons that the young person needs help (e.g. disruption in routine, school or family functioning). However, these reasons will not always be the same as those that motivate a young person to engage in treatment for OCD. It is for this reason that the clinician should carefully consider who is in the room while discussing goals. While it can be helpful to have a parent suggest useful goals, if they are not the same as the young person's and/or they are unable to express a difference of opinion, these goals may end up being that of the parent or therapist rather than those of the young person. This could potentially reduce motivation and result in difficulties during treatment. The problem with unclear or inaccurate goals is particularly apparent when it is time for the young person to translate what they have learnt about OCD into real-life experiments, such as stopping rituals in order to find out if their problem is about worry or real danger. If the young person views such tasks as particularly distressing, and cannot see how it would be useful to their life, they will be less inclined to carry out such experiments. With this is mind, it is often useful to see the young person alone, as well as with their parents, while creating goals.

When establishing goals, it is helpful for the young person and the therapist to break these into short, medium and long-term goals. Short-term goals involve tasks that the young person can achieve from session to session and begin working on immediately, such as understanding how OCD works or stopping particular rituals in order to find out if the problem is about worry or danger. In contrast, tasks that can be achieved by the end of treatment are described as medium-term goals and may include stopping all rituals, accepting intrusions as normal and allowing intrusions to remain in the mind. Compiling a list of goals can also clarify any misunderstandings that the young person may have about the way OCD works. For example, a young person who does not fully understand that intrusions are a normal part of life for everyone may be surprised to hear that treatment does not aim to get rid of all intrusive thoughts. Long-term goals involve dreams and hopes for a future that does not involve OCD. These can include things such as learning to drive, going to college or university, going travelling, being in a relationship or pursuing a particular career. It is important not to under-estimate the importance of long-term goals because some young people truly believe that many possibilities for the future are lost to them forever because of their OCD. Lost dreams and hopes may also be inadvertently reinforced by parents who verbally express fears about their child's future and what they believe the young person can or cannot do. It is important to address these limitations by rediscovering what kind of future the young person would like and to help them to understand that every goal for the short and medium term is an important stepping stone toward achieving their dreams and hopes for the future.

> It is important to establish the young person's short, medium and long-term goals.

Building an alternative view of the problem

By this point in therapy, the therapist and young person will have made sense of the problem and learned that OCD has been telling them that they need to do certain things to get rid of their worries. However, they will have started to consider the possibility that undertaking their solutions to the perceived danger (e.g. rituals, avoidance, looking for danger and reassurance seeking) actually keep their worry going by stopping them from finding out that their solutions are not responsible for preventing harm. It can be helpful at this point to suggest that OCD has been telling them that the world works in a certain way, but that actually it may work in a completely different way and that at the moment it is not really clear which is right. Up until now OCD will have been giving the young person the impression that their problem is about real danger, in that bad things are going to happen if they do not do their rituals. Introducing an alternative view, that their problem is about worry, can be more effective than trying to disprove their current OCD-driven 'danger' view and can then provide the backdrop for the remainder of treatment. Behavioural experiments and cognitive techniques can be designed to test out the evidence for these two opposing views of how their problem and the world really works.

Thus, the cognitive model of OCD can be simplified by writing two contrasting explanations about OCD that can be tested through experiments. The first, which is the explanation required for OCD to survive, might be written as follows: *The Problem is Danger: 'You truly are in danger from harm and you must do whatever you can to prevent this harm from happening.'* The second and alternative explanation would look something like this: *The Problem is Worry: 'You are a sensitive person who worries that things are more dangerous than they are and you try too hard to stop this worry. All the things OCD gets you to do make the worry worse.'* At this point in therapy it is helpful to encourage the young person to seriously consider each explanation by asking them if the problem really is about danger and they can prevent this harm, what should they do (i.e. carry out rituals)? In contrast, if the problem is about worrying that things are more dangerous than they actually are and trying too hard to make the worry go away, then what should they do (i.e. stop rituals)? It is important that each view and its ensuing actions are made as explicit as possible, so that the young person has a foundation on which to layer any new information gained from future experiments.

Therapist: It sounds as if OCD has been telling you that he knows how the world works and that if you don't do a habit or tell your mum, certain things are going to happen. Is that right?

Jack: Yes.

Therapist: Let's draw this out. Can you draw two columns and in the first one we'll write all the things that OCD says will happen if you don't do habits.

Jack: Okay, OCD says that I'll be a bad brother and that I could end up hurting Charlie by squashing him.

Therapist: And if you don't do what OCD says, what will happen to how worried you get?

Jack: It will go up and up and won't come down.

Therapist: No wonder you've been feeling so bad. Is there anything else OCD would predict?

Jack: I don't think so.

Therapist: Okay, so let's now think about a different way of thinking about this. This is the total opposite of what OCD says. What shall we call this?

Jack: Let's call this one 'Football King'!

Therapist: Okay, so what would Football King say would happen if you don't do a habit?

Jack: He would say OCD is a great big liar and that I'm a nice brother and that I'm not going to hurt Charlie. He would say you don't need to do habits and that you might be quite worried but after a while your worry would just disappear.

Therapist: Okay, so OCD says, 'Jack, if you don't do all these things, it means that you are a bad brother, you might hurt Charlie and that your worries will go up and up.' Is OCD saying that the

	problem here is danger and that if you don't do these things lots of bad stuff is going to happen?
Jack:	Yes.
Therapist:	But Football King says, 'OCD is a great big liar and that actually if you don't do a habit or tell your mum, you are not a bad brother and nothing will happen and actually your worry will go down.'
Jack:	Yes.
Therapist:	So, Football King says, 'You know what Jack, this isn't a problem about danger, this is actually a problem about worry.' [Pause.] Is that a new way of thinking about it, that the problem might actually be about worry rather than bad stuff happening?
Jack:	Yes.
Therapist:	And what would it mean if OCD is right?
Jack:	I need to do habits.
Therapist:	And if Football King is right?
Jack:	Habits are a waste of time – maybe I should be having fun instead.
Therapist:	What do you think about that idea?
Jack:	That would be good.
Therapist:	So how do we find out if OCD is right or if Football King is right?
Jack:	I could not do a habit and see what happens.
Therapist:	That sounds like a good place to start.

It is useful at this point to ask the young person to rate their belief in each explanation on a scale from 0 to 100 (with 0 being 'I do not believe it at all' and 100 being 'I completely believe this'). Throughout treatment the therapist can then ask the young person to re-rate their beliefs. The next stage in treatment involves building on this belief by asking the young person to consider all possible evidence to support both explanations. It is often easier to start collecting evidence in favour of the problem being danger. However, it is not uncommon for a young person to struggle to find any evidence at all. This realisation can help loosen their belief about the world being a dangerous place, while simultaneously building the belief that their problem might be about worry. In doing so, it is very important to make sure that all evidence is considered, no matter how small or unlikely (e.g. forgetting to pray one night and falling ill the next day or a loved one being in an accident or having a strong emotional feeling that the danger is real). All of this evidence provides a focus for treatment and an opportunity to consider alternative explanations (for example, challenging a young person's belief that they are responsible for the accident to their family member).

Once a clear list of evidence for their problem being danger has been collected, it is helpful to move on to evidence for the idea that their problem is about worry. Useful questions to pose to the young person include:

- Have there been times when you did not carry out a ritual and nothing happened?
- Have you ever had a thought about harm followed by nothing happening?
- Has your worry become better or worse since carrying out rituals?
- What was your worry like before you had OCD?
- Have you ever noticed that in the long term the OCD gets worse when you do the things it wants?
- Have you ever carried out a ritual and it did not work?

> Introducing an alternative view of the problem as being around 'worry' rather than 'danger' can be helpful in giving the young person a different way of making sense of what is going on.

Behavioural experiments

By this stage in treatment, belief in the problem being danger should be loosening, and the belief in the problem being worry should be growing. This loosening of belief in danger can increase the motivation required to move from discussion-focused therapy toward real-life experiments. These experiments are designed to provide stronger evidence within the heart (i.e. at an emotional level) supporting the notion that the problem is worry rather than real danger. Thus, the purpose of carrying out experiments is to help the young person build up a body of evidence to support a new way of thinking about their problem (i.e. that they worry too much about danger) while decreasing evidence for their previously held interpretation of the problem (i.e. that they truly are in danger and responsible for causing or preventing this danger). When introducing experiments, it is useful to describe them as a way of finding out how the world really works, rather than how they think it works. Stories and imagery can be a useful method to get this idea across. For example, you can compare carrying out experiments to a scientist trying to find out how the world really works by doing experiments in their lab instead of simply relying on what other people say. This can then be presented to the young person as an image of a courtroom with evidence for and against being presented and examined. It can be useful to use role play to bring this idea to life, especially when working with younger children.

When setting up the first experiment with the young person it is important to help them choose something that is likely to be successful and something that can be tested immediately (e.g. testing whether they can make something happen in the room by thinking it to test out the idea that thinking things implies they have control over what will actually happen). It may be necessary for the therapist to model the experiment (or something more anxiety provoking) to the young person first if they are finding it difficult to engage in the experiment. The therapist should bear in mind that any experiments they carry out should be designed to model that they are trying to gain new information and that this may produce some degree of anxiety, but the anxiety is manageable and decreases over time. The therapist should try to model that they do experience some anxiety. Thought should therefore be given to choosing an experiment that does in fact produce some anxiety for the therapist (e.g. thinking about a loved one dying or rubbing an item of food on the bottom of their shoe before eating it). When setting up experiments it is also important that the young person is clear about the purpose of the experiment. Prior to conducting the experiment the therapist should ask the young person what it is they are trying to test out, what their predictions are and what the results would indicate about OCD if their predictions were found to be true or not true. Consideration should also be given to what future action the potential findings would suggest the young person takes.

> 'I can't let you do this until I know for sure that you understand why we are doing it. It is not to punish or torture you, but to help us find out how this problem really works. That is, to find out if the problem is worry rather than danger. Can you tell me in your own words why you are about to do this and what it might tell you about OCD and the way forward?'

As treatment progresses it is important to encourage the young person to come up with their own experiments. Not only can this build motivation and engagement, but it also helps to ensure that the young person is not obtaining reassurance from the therapist by shifting responsibility for danger away from themselves (e.g. 'If something goes wrong it is not my fault because my therapist told me to do it.'). Consequently, it is important that over time the young person takes on increasing amounts of responsibility. The following structure can be a useful starting point in terms of carrying out experiments and gradually shifting responsibility toward the young person:

1   The therapist comes up with an idea and also carries it out. The young person copies this.
2   The therapist comes up with an idea, but does not carry it out. The young person does this.
3   The young person comes up with an idea and carries it out in front of the therapist.
4   The young person comes up with an idea, does not tell the therapist, and carries it out.
5   The young person comes up with an idea, does not tell the therapist, and only discusses the results.

Experiments should only be carried out if they fit the needs of the young person according to their beliefs. For example, a young person who believes that thoughts can cause harm would benefit from experiments focusing on thought–action fusion. For example, to see if thinking something can make it happen, the young person could think of the therapist being hit by a car as the therapist goes outside and walks around the car park. However, such an experiment would be of little value to a young person who does not believe that thoughts can cause harm. Examples of various experiments are set out in Appendix E. However, it is important to remember that they are a guide only and that many great experiments have been thought of in the midst of a difficult treatment session.

- Behavioural experiments are an essential part of treatment and are designed to provide evidence to support a new way of thinking about the problem.
- Experiments must always clearly relate to the specific beliefs of the young person.

Common obstacles to treatment

Helping the young person to engage with a different understanding of their OCD and to start to engage with experiments can be an issue that arises early on in treatment. It is important to try and identify the young person's individual reasons for not wanting to engage in treatment and then help them to move forward on these issues. For example, if the young person feels that their OCD is not really a problem for them, the therapist should help them consider the pros and cons of their OCD, making sure they give enough time to the pros before moving on to the cons and then reviewing the evidence for the perceived pros.

Engagement can also be hindered if the young person appears to resent being offered help. If this appears to be the case it can be helpful to find out what it means to them to receive help (e.g. they are weak, stupid, or unable to sort things out for themselves) and to challenge this with questions such as: 'What do you think it means if you need some help?' 'Do you think you are the only one that needs help with something?' 'Can you think of a time when someone in your family or a friend needed help with something?' If after the reason for not wanting to engage has been identified and challenged the young person is still reluctant to begin treatment, it can be useful to review whether they feel their way of handling the OCD has been working. Try and gain minimal engagement (e.g. for a short period of time or for one area or ritual) to see if there may be a better way of handling things. The therapist can assure the young person that if they are not happy with the other way of dealing with things, they will put all their effort into helping the young person go back to doing it the obsessional way again.

One of the most common difficulties encountered in treatment is when the young person refuses to give experiments a go. It is vital that the therapist does not take an authoritarian stance and try to push the young person to do the experiment as this may threaten their engagement. Instead it is important to identify collaboratively what it is that is feeling so difficult and then try to problem-solve or get the young person to review the evidence for their worry. It is vital that the young person feels they are in control of what is going on within treatment. However, the challenge for the therapist is to allow this to occur whilst also encouraging the young person to step slightly outside their comfort zone to gain new information. Thus, the most common reason for not wanting to take part in an experiment is because it feels too scary or too great a leap for the young person to take. If this is the case, the therapist and young person should consider taking a step back and think about carrying out an experiment that is less anxiety provoking.

However, it is also important that the therapist is not overly cautious as young people with OCD are often ready and able to make some huge leaps and therefore gain invaluable new evidence. It can be helpful to use natural opportunities whenever they arise. For example, if a young person spontaneously suggests an experiment, then briefly review the reason for carrying it out and go with it immediately. It can also be helpful to remind the young person that it is sometimes better to do something you are scared of straightaway rather than think it through too much and have them find examples of this in their own life to build motivation. Similarly, it is helpful to highlight the nature of anxiety and the fact that things often are not as bad as they initially seem and to encourage the young person to identify previous non-OCD examples of times when they have been really worried about something but it has actually turned out to be manageable. Where possible, the therapist should try to make experiments fun, for example, if a young person enjoys tennis then incorporate this into experiments. If you are carrying out an experiment showing that focusing on body symptoms increases their salience, you may want to alternate between focusing on body symptoms and asking the young person to give you a quick verbal tennis lesson. Finally, if it becomes apparent that the experiment was too difficult for the young person, it is important that the therapist takes responsibility for the situation that has arisen to avoid the young person losing motivation. For example, 'It seems I have made a bit of a mistake here as I don't think we should have tried this experiment quite yet. Let's try something else now instead – what do you suggest?'

An additional reason why young people stop engaging in behavioural experiments is if they are constantly discounting results from them and therefore do not see the purpose of trying any more experiments. For example, they may think of harm and it does not occur and rather than conclude that thoughts do not cause harm, they may dismiss these results. If this occurs the therapist should cease trying to get the young person to conduct experiments that focus on disproving danger and instead shift to discussion and experiments that focus on proving the problem is worry (i.e. the more you do your rituals, the more you worry, and the more you argue with OCD and listen to his lies and discounting, the more you worry, so it is better to stop listening to him completely and stop rituals and just carry on with life).

Another common obstacle to treatment success is when the young person has started to make some positive changes but then gets to the stage where they do not want to push on any further in case they 'rock the boat and things go wrong'. In this instance it can be useful to use the analogy of 'digging weeds out of the garden', whereby the therapist asks the young person what problems they can see with someone just mowing over weeds in their garden to get rid of them (i.e. they will keep growing back). The therapist should ask the young person what they think would be a better solution to the weeds (such as pulling them out by the roots) and then help them to consider how this might relate to their OCD (i.e. unless they keep going and get right to the roots and really disprove the OCD it is likely to creep back in). Thus, despite some improvement the young person might complain that they are still bothered by intrusive thoughts about harm and responsibility. In this situation, it is quite possible that they are still carrying out rituals on occasion and the therapist should ask the young person if this is the case, for example, 'You have been doing really well in therapy so far, but I have just started to wonder if perhaps OCD is still getting you to do back-up rituals every once in a while. Do you think this could be happening?' Then ask 'What could be the problem with doing back-up rituals?' 'Why do you think I am concerned about the idea of you doing any back-up rituals at all, no matter how small?' This encourages the young person to consider that this may stop them from completely finding out that they are not responsible for preventing harm.

Another strategy that can be helpful if motivation to (continue to) change becomes an issue is to go back to the young person's goals and remind them that every little thing they do is actually helping them move along the path toward achieving their goals. It can be especially useful to refer back to the longer term goals as these relate to the young person's dreams of what life would and could be like if OCD was eradicated from their life. Additional strategies such as reviewing the pros and cons or conducting a 'cost-benefit analysis' of staying as they are or attempting more things can also be helpful when trying to build motivation for further change.

> If the young person appears unwilling to engage in treatment it is important to take a step back and address this.

Creating a blueprint and developing a setback plan

A blueprint of therapy aims to help the young person pull together what they have learnt about how their OCD works and the strategies that have been helpful in trying to eradicate OCD from their life. A blueprint also aims to plan for setbacks that the young person may encounter once treatment has come to an end. Creative techniques such as doing a documentary style video or doing a collage can be useful in helping the young person summarise treatment in this way. The therapist should begin with briefly reviewing the history of the young person's OCD and how it took hold of them. This can be done verbally by asking the young person to talk about their formulation of OCD or by asking the young person about their understanding of when and why things started to go wrong. It is helpful to reiterate that OCD took over due to their faulty beliefs (about the meaning of the intrusions) and them coming up with solutions that ultimately became the problem.

The therapist should then introduce the idea of setbacks to the young person and if possible should try to inoculate the young person against failure by normalising the occurrence of setbacks and reframing them as an opportunity to practise the strategies they have learnt in therapy. It can be helpful to strengthen the young person's belief in their own ability to beat the OCD by reviewing experiments and homework they have carried out, by highlighting the fact that most of the work has been conducted by them between sessions and by reminding them of their successes by revisiting their goals. The therapist and the young person can then work on the setback plan and whilst doing so the therapist should remember to continue to bring the young person's focus back to what the strategy would tell them about how the problem and the world works (i.e. that ultimately the problem is about worry and therefore does not require them to take any further action). Topics to put in the setback plan include information on any:

- personal triggers for their OCD
- possible stressors that may exacerbate symptoms
- early warning signs that OCD may be creeping back into their life
- strategies to cope with early warning signs (e.g. refusing to do what OCD wants, doing the opposite, going over the top to really show OCD who is boss)
- preventative solutions to keep OCD at bay (e.g. do one dirty thing every day, say something violent every day, just to spite OCD, intentionally put one thing out of place everyday, etc.).

- Treatment should end by pulling together what has been learnt in treatment and by developing a setback plan with the young person.
- Setbacks should be reframed as normal and an opportunity to practise strategies learned in therapy.

5

CBT with younger children

Linda J. Atkinson

Children as young as seven or eight years of age are able to benefit from CBT (Cartwright-Hatton *et al.*, 2004). Further, Stallard (2005) has argued that children as young as five may also benefit from CBT, given adaptations to content and presentation (Doherr *et al.*, 2005; Flavell *et al.*, 2001; Wellman *et al.*, 1996). As an example, Tolin (2001) reported the use of techniques such as externalising OCD, bibliotherapy and parental involvement in the treatment of a five-year-old child with OCD.

Children under the age of about ten years are most likely to be seen with a caregiver during treatment. While the general structure of the treatment follows that for older children and adolescents (i.e. psychoeducation, changing beliefs, changing behaviour and relapse prevention), adaptations include a greater use of humour, simpler language and a need to ensure that the family's beliefs are acknowledged and managed (see also Chapter 7). Working with young children with OCD usually requires more extensive education about OCD than is required for older children.

Engaging the child and their family

Young children may need longer to establish a successful working partnership with the therapist, which will often be facilitated through a parent. They are often used to being taught rather than discovering things for themselves so encouraging the child to take charge of as many tasks as possible during therapy helps them take an active role (e.g. asking the child to hang the engaged sign on the door). Using humour and asking the child for their ideas on how to make treatment fun will also encourage participation.

Many children do not know why they have come to the clinic. The explanation can usefully be combined with discovering the child's knowledge of OCD, their expectations of treatment and then explaining what treatment is and is not. The therapist explains that CBT involves finding out how OCD works and learning better ways of dealing with the problem. Parents should also be told that there are many ways that they can support their child throughout treatment. For example, parents can attend treatment sessions, learn how their child's OCD works, model helpful behaviours (e.g. if a parent values cleanliness they could focus on becoming less clean), develop a plan for managing requests for reassurance or encourage the child to come up with their own solutions (rather than solving problems for the child).

Introducing therapy

After a brief explanation of what OCD stands for and what obsessions and compulsions are, the therapist starts to develop a description of the child's OCD. The child's understanding should be checked throughout by asking them to explain it back to the therapist. Displaying the information on a flipchart helps to fix the ideas in the child's mind and enables them to take things home as a reminder of the session's content. The therapist should explain that CBT is short for cognitive behaviour therapy, which is an adult phrase that means doing things and thinking in new ways that will help to get rid of OCD. It is important to tell the child that CBT does not mean going to hospital or taking pills or medicine (unless the child is already). It does however mean that the therapist will ask lots of questions, that it works best when the child, therapist and family work together as a team, and that the child will have to practise at home.

The therapist will then explain how common OCD is. For teenagers, it may be sufficient to provide prevalence rates, but in younger age groups it helps to give concrete examples. For example, the therapist can ask the child how many other children in their school might have OCD (e.g. in a school of 1000 pupils at least ten other children have OCD). The therapist might then ask if the child is surprised by the numbers of fellow sufferers, and why other children do not talk about it.

> - Children as young as five may benefit from CBT, given adaptations to content and presentation.
> - While the general structure of the treatment follows that for older children, adaptations include simpler language, a greater use of stories, metaphors, role plays and humour, more extensive education and a need to ensure that the family's beliefs are acknowledged and managed.

Beginning to make sense of the problem

Thinking about OCD as a bully

As described in Chapter 4, the aim of the first treatment session is to introduce the cognitive model of OCD. With younger children, a simple way is to compare OCD to a bully. Most children know that bullies are mean, scare people and try to make them do things that they don't want to do (e.g. give away their money or toys). OCD is similar because OCD is mean, it scares people and makes children do things they don't want to do (e.g. rituals). The therapist can ask:

- What do you know about bullies?
- How do bullies make people feel: happy, cheerful or scared?
- What sort of things do bullies do to make people feel scared (e.g. threaten to hit you)?
- What happens if you give in to a bully?

These concepts can be illustrated by role playing a bully and demanding that the child gives them one pound. The therapist then asks the child what will happen the next day when the bully sees you at school (e.g. the bully will ask you for money again)? Then the therapist asks the child:

- If giving in to a bully makes the bully worse, what is the thing to do to stop a bully?

The child should be encouraged to think about standing up to or ignoring the bully so that the bully realises there is no point in continuing to behave in this way, as they are not going to get what they want. Once the child understands how a bully works, they are asked how OCD might be the same as a bully. The child's knowledge of their own OCD is then explored so as to enhance the comparison, for example:

- How does OCD make you feel?
- What does OCD say will happen if you don't do what it says?
- What sorts of things does OCD make you do?
- What happens the next day when you give in to OCD, does OCD get worse?
- Do rituals make OCD come back and bother you again and again?
- What do you need to do to stop OCD?
- If you stand up to OCD, what do you think you might you find out about OCD's lies?

Reviewing a recent example of OCD

A key task of CBT is to develop a formulation of the problem so that the child and their parents can make sense of what is happening. However, more time needs to be taken with younger children to help the child identify beliefs associated with intrusive thoughts, that is, how the child thinks about their thinking. The therapist can introduce this exercise by explaining that the best way to beat OCD is to uncover OCD's secrets and lies by talking about him. It is often helpful to provide a younger child with information rather than engaging in guided discovery. For example, rather than asking the child 'What do you think this thought meant?', the therapist may say:

> 'Sometimes OCD tells us that if we have a thought like this it means it is going to come true. So if someone had a thought of their mum getting ill and dying, OCD would tell them that it meant that she would get ill and die unless they did something to stop it. I wondered if this is what it says to you?'.

To ensure that the belief acknowledged by the child is a genuine belief that they hold, the therapist can then ask the child to elaborate on the belief by asking 'How come you believe this?' and 'What makes you think this?'

It is common for young children to struggle to recall a recent incident. If this occurs, parents may be able to help the child remember. The therapist can then check with the child that it is a good example. Throughout, the therapist writes up a shared understanding of how the child's OCD works, using the child's own words. Figure 5.1 shows the formulation for Dan, a ten-year-old boy who repeatedly engages in covert rituals (e.g. imagining monsters in his mind) whenever he worries about his mother coming to harm.

The following transcript from Dan's first therapy session demonstrates the process of developing a formulation. The therapist pretends to be the student in order to learn about OCD from Dan, who becomes the teacher:

> *Therapist:* What was the very first sign that let you know OCD was around?
>
> *Dan:* I couldn't find Mum and I thought that she might be hurt.
>
> *Therapist:* So a scary a thought about your mum suddenly popped into your head all on its own?
>
> *Dan:* Yes.
>
> *Therapist:* What kind of harm did you imagine could happen to your mum?
>
> *Dan:* Someone might hurt her with a knife.
>
> *Therapist:* That sounds pretty scary. Thank you for telling me about this scary thought. It will help us to beat OCD. Let's write down your scary thought in a box called 'intrusive thoughts' [the therapist asks Dan to write or draw an image of 'My mum might be hurt with a knife'].
>
> *Therapist:* Do you know why I called this thought an intrusive thought?
>
> *Dan:* No.
>
> *Therapist:* Intrusive thoughts are words or pictures that suddenly pop into your mind all on their own. You don't want them to come

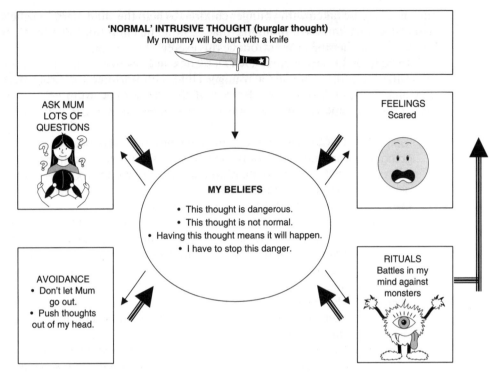

Figure 5.1   Shared understanding of Dan's OCD

into your mind, but they come in anyway. Intrusive thoughts are like burglars who come into people's houses without asking. Did your thought about harm come into your mind all on its own, without asking?

Dan: Yes.

Therapist: Okay, so this thought about mum was an intrusive thought. I want you to watch me closely now because I am going to write the word 'normal' next to 'intrusive thoughts' on our picture [Figure 5.1]. How come I am calling your intrusive burglar thoughts 'normal'?

Dan: I don't know.

Therapist: Because it is normal to have upsetting thoughts come into your mind. Everyone has scary intrusive thoughts that come into their heads. It is normal. I will talk to you more about this later, but right now I want to find out why you are so upset by your normal intrusive burglar thoughts. When this intrusive thought about harm popped into your head, what made you so scared about it?

Dan: I had to do a mind-battle (e.g. fight imaginary monsters in my mind).

Therapist: I am going to slow you down a bit because you are my teacher and I have to make sure I really understand how your

OCD works. When you had the thought about harm coming to your mum, what did you imagine could be the worst possible thing that could happen?

Dan: Someone might hurt her and she could die.

Therapist: That sounds really scary. I think I understand your OCD much better now. It seems that the reason you were very upset about these thoughts is because you believe that having these thoughts means that your mum really could die. I think I would get upset too if I believed the same thing as you. But I am curious about something? When you had the thought that your mum could be harmed, did you think that this was a normal thought?

Dan: No, because no one else has these thoughts.

Therapist: Can I ask you another question? When this thought about something bad happening to your mum popped into your mind, did you think that having this thought could make it happen?

Dan: Yes.

Therapist: How does that work exactly?

Dan: Well why would I think about Mum being hurt, if it was not going to happen?

Therapist: So far I have learnt that the reason why you were so upset about thoughts of harm coming into your mind is because you believe that having these thoughts is not normal and that these thoughts are a sign that harm will happen. Is that right, or do I have it a bit wrong?

Dan: That's right.

Therapist: How much do you believe this from 0 to 10 (0 = I don't believe, 10 = I completely believe).

Dan: 10. I totally believe it.

Therapist: When you had these beliefs, did you feel as if you had to do something?

Dan: I cried and then had to do a mind-battle in my head.

Therapist: Can you please teach me, as your student, what that this battle (ritual) looked like and what you had to do?

Dan: I imagined killing monsters with a machine gun.

Therapist: Why did you have to win?

Dan: Because if I didn't win, it would be like letting bad things happen to Mum, and then I would be sure that bad things would happen.

Therapist: It seems that you believe that you must do mind-battles to stop bad things from happening to your mum. Is that right? [Dan nods.] This might be another belief that we need to write down.

Having identified the child's beliefs, the therapist explores their effect on emotional reactions, avoidance, reassurance seeking and selective attention.

For young children it is often necessary to provide examples of what each question means. For example, when asking a child how their thoughts made them feel, it is helpful to show them some pictures of possible emotions (e.g. scared, worried, frightened, happy, angry). When asking about avoidance, it can help if the therapist gives examples of different avoidance strategies (e.g. pushing thoughts away, moving away from people or things that scare you, emptying your mind, trying hard not to be alone). As soon as the therapist has been able to identify: (a) the child's intrusion; (b) how the intrusion has been interpreted; (c) the effects of these beliefs, the therapist summarises what has been learnt about OCD and importantly emphasises that the problem is not the intrusion, but is what the child thinks the intrusion means. To consolidate the learning, the child is then asked to explain in their own words what they have learnt.

- When introducing the cognitive model of OCD to younger children, it can be helpful to compare OCD to a bully.

- With young children, a formulation is important, but more time is taken to introduce the task and to help the child identify beliefs associated with intrusive thoughts.

- When developing the formulation, it can be helpful for the therapist to take on the role of student to learn about OCD from the child.

- It may be necessary to provide examples of what questions mean and use pictures to think about emotions associated with OCD.

The vicious cycle of OCD: the itchy bite metaphor

As part of the preparation for behaviour change, the therapist attempts to loosen the child's belief in the usefulness of rituals and other unhelpful strategies by discussing whether the child's solutions might be making the problem worse rather than better. For example, when looking at Dan's diagram of OCD (Figure 5.1), the therapist may ask the following questions:

- Have you ever wondered, even for a little bit, if the things you do such as rituals and pushing your thoughts away might make the worry worse rather than better?
- Has your worry become bigger or smaller since you started doing rituals?
- If your worry has been getting bigger, does this mean that your rituals are making the problem better or worse?

A useful metaphor for rituals is the *itchy bite*, because most children know that scratching an itchy bite makes the itching worse later. This metaphor can be brought to life by acting it out. The therapist draws a red dot on their own arm and begins to scratch it while asking the child, 'How do I feel while I scratch this itchy bite?' (i.e. better and relieved), 'But then what happens to the itchy bite?' (i.e. it gets bigger, redder and itchier). At this point, the therapist draws a larger itchy bite on their arm and asks the child, 'Now that the itchy bite is larger, what do I want to do even more?' (i.e. scratch it). The therapist then asks if the scratching solution is making the itchy bite better or worse. The therapist might then suggest that the rituals might be similar to scratching and could ask the child if the rituals are making the problem better or worse.

> The itchy bite metaphor can highlight how the child's rituals and other strategies can make their OCD worse.

Normalising intrusive thoughts

As with adolescents, one way of normalising intrusive thoughts with younger children is to provide examples of intrusive thoughts, such as those of the therapist and the parent. Often when the child realises that their thoughts are normal, their distress is reduced and the need to ritualise may also reduce. To show how common intrusive thoughts are, the therapist can draw a circle to represent all the people in the world. Both the child and parent are asked to show how many people in the world have intrusive thoughts by colouring part of the circle. Children and parents typically colour a quarter to three quarters of the circle. The therapist then explains that lots of people in the world have been asked if they have intrusive thoughts and around 90 per cent say they do, which means nearly all the circle should be coloured in. The child is encouraged to reflect on this new information by answering the following questions:

- Are you surprised that so many people have intrusive thoughts?
- Did you know that it is usual to have these thoughts?
- What is it like to find out you are like others?
- If your intrusive thoughts are normal, do you have to fix them?
- What do you do when you have other intrusive thoughts (i.e. carry on doing what anyone would do and leave the thought alone)?
- Does OCD try to make you think you are not normal?
- Why is OCD a liar for making you think that?

> Normalising intrusive thoughts is an essential part of therapy and pictures can be used to demonstrate this with younger children.

Changing beliefs about the meaning of intrusive thoughts

Reappraising what it means to have intrusive thoughts

Children with OCD need to reinterpret their intrusive thoughts as meaning that they 'care' rather than as a sign of 'danger'. This can be achieved by carrying out a role play where the therapist pretends to be a professional killer who does not care about people's lives. The therapist pretends to receive a letter and reads out loud the name of the person to be killed, 'I must kill Johnnie Bonnie today at 12 pm.' The therapist then pretends to happily read the newspaper while having a thought that they will kill someone. The therapist asks the child why the trained killer is not upset or bothered by the thought of killing someone. Discussion focuses on the idea that the trained killer is not upset because he is a horrible person who does not care about life or death. The therapist then pretends to be a loving kind mother who has had a stressful day with her children. The mother suddenly has a thought of killing her children and is a bit upset by this thought. The child is asked if the mother is upset by the thought of killing her children because (a) the mother is a horrible nasty person who wants to kill her children or (b) because the mother really cares and loves her children. Discussion focuses on the idea that noticing intrusive thoughts means we care.

> Children with OCD need to learn to reinterpret their intrusive thoughts as meaning that they care, rather than a sign of danger. This can be illustrated by the therapist carrying out a role play pretending to be a trained killer.

Understanding that thoughts are not enough to cause harm

Many young people believe that thoughts and urges are extremely important and should not be ignored because they can directly lead to harm. For example, Samia was a nine-year-old girl with repetitive intrusive thoughts and urges around touching her sister's genitals. She believed that these thoughts and urges would cause her to behave sexually inappropriately unless she carried out rituals to prevent this from happening. The therapist illustrated how Samia was seeing these thoughts as overly important by drawing a dot on a piece of paper and describing this dot as an upsetting thought or urge that suddenly flew into her mind. At the bottom of the page the therapist wrote down the feared outcome (e.g. I will do sexual things to my sister). The therapist then pointed to the 'dot' and asked Samia, 'Does OCD try to make you believe that this little thought is enough to make harm happen?' The therapist then drew an arrow from the thought all the way down to the feared outcome to emphasise the unhelpful belief that thoughts can directly cause harm. The therapist then planted a seed of doubt into

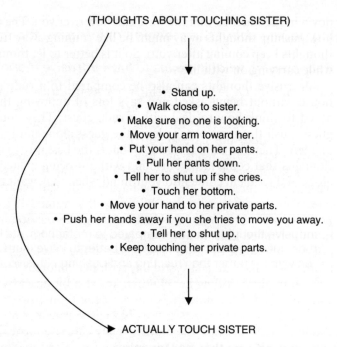

(THOUGHTS ABOUT TOUCHING SISTER)

- Stand up.
- Walk close to sister.
- Make sure no one is looking.
- Move your arm toward her.
- Put your hand on her pants.
- Pull her pants down.
- Tell her to shut up if she cries.
- Touch her bottom.
- Move your hand to her private parts.
- Push her hands away if you she tries to move you away.
- Tell her to shut up.
- Keep touching her private parts.

ACTUALLY TOUCH SISTER

Figure 5.2   Thoughts are not enough to cause harm

Samia's mind by asking her if she was really sure that thoughts are enough to make bad things happen and then getting Samia to consider all the things that actually need to happen in order to turn a thought or urge into action (see Figure 5.2). These actions were written in a long list directly underneath the dot representing her thought. Samia was then asked what she thought the diagram showed. Discussion focuses on the idea that thoughts are not enough to cause harm because so many other more important things need to happen.

> It is also important to learn that thoughts alone are not enough to cause harm and that many other important things need to happen.

Treating thoughts as meaningless

Another issue to consider is what other people do with intrusive thoughts. The goal is to help the child realise that it is better to leave intrusive thoughts alone and to carry on with life rather than reacting and pushing intrusive thoughts away. Useful metaphors for managing intrusive thoughts include '*the wave*' and '*the rude guest*'. If a child is familiar with ocean waves, it can be helpful to ask the child what happens if you try to run away from big waves (i.e. the wave may pick you up or knock you over). It is better to duck down in the water so that the wave can flow over you. The child is then asked how pushing thoughts away might be like running away from a wave (i.e. the thoughts keep coming after you). So it is better to let thoughts flow over you while carrying on with life.

Intrusive thoughts can also be compared to a rude guest who visits a house without being asked and says lots of annoying things. The child is asked to think how to deal with a rude guest. They could argue with the guest, push the guest out, or leave the guest alone until they became bored and left. Then the child is asked, 'What is the best way to deal with intrusive thoughts that come into your mind without being invited?' (leave thoughts alone and let them come into your mind when they want to).

> Intrusive thoughts can be compared to metaphors, such as waves or a rude guest, in order to see that it is better to leave them alone and carry on with life rather than reacting and pushing intrusive thoughts away.

Introducing an alternative explanation

The possibility of an alternative non-threatening explanation for the OCD is then introduced. A simple way is to ask the child to *become a detective* to find out whether OCD is telling the truth or is a liar. Both explanations are written on a piece of paper and the child is asked to rate their belief in each explanation on a scale from 0 to 10 (0 = I do not believe it at all, 10 = I completely believe it). The process of undermining the child's belief in OCD and building motivation to carry out experiments can begin by asking the child to compile evidence for both explanations (see Figure 5.3).

Carrying out behavioural experiments

Even quite young children will know about experiments. Young children find them helpful because they demonstrate in a concrete way that they do not have to continue doing what OCD tells them. They are encouraged to think that experiments can find out if OCD is telling the truth or lies. If the child does not understand the concept of experiments it is helpful to describe some. For example, to test a belief like 'all dogs kill people' the child and therapist might design a few experiments such as: visit a pet shop with dogs, stand near a friend's dog, pat a dog, or take a dog for a walk. As soon as the child and therapist have designed some experiments, the child is asked what these experiments could teach someone who believed that 'all dogs kill' (e.g. not all dogs kill, dogs can be friendly). When designing experiments for

OCD IS TELLING THE TRUTH (belief = 9/10)	OCD IS TELLING LIES (belief = 3/10)
• Intrusive thoughts mean bad things will happen. • I have to stop bad thoughts from happening. • My rituals stop bad things. • Rituals make my worry go away.	• Intrusive thoughts are normal. Everyone gets bad thoughts. • I do not have to stop bad thoughts. • Rituals do not work. • Rituals make my worry stay.
EVIDENCE FOR OCD TELLING THE TRUTH	EVIDENCE FOR OCD BEING A LIAR
• I had a bad thought about my neighbour and then he died. • I thought about winning a computer game then I won. • I didn't do my rituals and then Daddy hurt his leg. • I didn't wash my hands and I got sick one day. • Nothing has happened yet because I do rituals.	• Sometimes I have thoughts and they don't come true. • When I was really little I didn't do rituals and everyone was fine. • Sometimes I forget to do my rituals and nothing happens. • Last week I ate a biscuit without washing my hands properly and I did not die.

Figure 5.3   Two explanations

OCD, the therapist needs to have a clear idea about the child's OCD-related beliefs in order to tailor them to specific beliefs, for example:

- thoughts can make things happen
- bad thoughts mean I am a bad person
- germs will definitely kill me
- I am the only one with this kind of thought
- rituals make me feel better and stop harm
- it is up to me to stop bad things from happening.

Treatment sessions should involve the following:

- identify an unhelpful belief
- set up two opposing explanations (i.e. OCD is telling the truth or OCD is a liar)
- ask the child to rate their current belief on a scale from 0 to 10
- ask the child to make predictions based on the two explanations
- carry out the experiment
- afterwards, discuss the results.

For example, a child who believes that reciting words in his head keeps his mother safe could be asked how much he believes that this is really true (i.e. rituals stop harm coming to Mum). The strength of the child's belief could be loosened by asking the child to describe exactly how their rituals work and to recall every single time that their mother has been harmed because of their failure to do rituals. The child could also be asked to recall what has happened when they have not carried out their rituals. The usefulness of rituals can be challenged by asking the child what they think a policeman should do if he sees something bad happening: that is, should the policeman (a) carry out rituals and walk away? or (b) do something to help such as protect a child and run after the criminal?

- Experiments allow the young person to become a detective and find out whether OCD is telling the truth or is a liar and demonstrate in a concrete way that the young person does not have to continue doing what OCD tells them.
- When designing experiments, the therapist needs to have a clear idea about the child's OCD-related beliefs.

Once a child's belief has been loosened, they may be motivated to carry out experiments. For example, the usefulness of these rituals could be tested by asking the child to carry out the ritual (i.e. recite special words) in the session to prevent their mother getting hurt. The therapist then tells the child that they will throw a pen at their mother's leg. The child's task is to prevent their mother being hurt by carrying out the ritual. The child is asked what should happen if OCD is telling the truth about rituals stopping harm (i.e. the pen should not hurt his mother) and what should happen if OCD is telling lies about rituals stopping harm (i.e. the pen will hurt his mother). The development of more helpful beliefs can be consolidated by helping the child think through the results by asking questions such as:

- What have you learnt from this experiment?
- If OCD is telling the truth what should have happened?
- Now that you know that OCD is a liar, do you have to do what OCD tells you to do?
- The next time OCD tells you to do a ritual, what will you tell OCD?
- How much do you believe now that rituals stop harm?

Usually children will cooperate with experiments if they are done swiftly using humour and enthusiasm to reduce anxiety and prevent refusal. Many children are initially reluctant to carry out experiments and this can be managed by the therapist modelling difficult experiments (e.g. for children with contamination fears the therapist touches the bottom of their shoe and then wipes their face) followed by suggesting an easier experiment for the child (e.g. the child touches the phone and the computer). The therapist should avoid stand-offs with the child over experiments. If a child refuses to do an experiment, it may be wise to back down and move on to another experiment. As the child's confidence increases, the therapist can return to the previously refused experiment.

> Many young children are initially reluctant to carry out experiments and this can be managed by the therapist modelling difficult experiments and carrying them out swiftly, using humour and novelty.

Throughout treatment it is important that the therapist is aware of the possibility that the child may be passing responsibility on to adults while carrying out experiments. This is a problem because it stops the child from discovering that things would have been okay whether or not the therapist and/or their parents were in the room. If a child has shifted responsibility to other adults, the therapist should arrange to have several treatment sessions alone with the child and encourage the child to design and carry out experiments on their own. Examples of different experiments are listed in Appendix E.

The therapist should not feel limited to carrying out experiments in the office. Field trips can address problems that are not readily available in the office and help generalise treatment gains to other settings. Field trips can take place wherever OCD causes problems, including the child's home, school, public toilets, cafeterias, public transport, swimming pools, dirty places and busy streets. During home visits the child can show the therapist around their house and point out where OCD bothers them. The child is then asked to act as if OCD is their best friend and to do everything that OCD tells them to do. When this has been completed, the child is asked to re-enact the day as if they hate OCD and to refuse to do anything that OCD wants them to do. The aim of this task is to help the child to realise:

- that it feels better to act normally rather than doing rituals
- that it is easier to stand up to OCD than previously thought
- that they do not have to do rituals to feel okay
- that OCD is a liar because nothing bad happens when they stop doing rituals.

> Field trips can address problems that are not readily available in the office and generalise treatment gains to other settings.

Voicing intrusive thoughts

Once the child understands that it is normal to have intrusive thoughts, they are encouraged to repeat intrusive thoughts out loud. The rationale for this is to help the child discover that it really is okay to have these thoughts and that having them on purpose might even make them disappear more quickly. For example, while the child is repeating obsessional thoughts the therapist may ask the child to let them know when another thought already wants to take its place (e.g. a thought about what they want for dinner tonight or how bored they are or if they feel a muscle ache). The child is then encouraged to consider what it means if another thought just pops in and takes over the original intrusive thoughts (e.g. you don't need to control your thoughts because they eventually disappear and are replaced by new thoughts).

Finding out whether arguing with OCD works

Mental arguing occurs when a young person tries to think their way out of a worry by arguing mentally with the worry. For example, Samia tried to cope with her worry by constantly arguing 'for' and 'against' the possibility of touching her sister in sexual ways. Mental arguing is unhelpful because it increases intrusive thoughts and doubts and intensifies beliefs about danger. This can be illustrated by comparing an argument in your mind to arguing with a three-year-old child who wants something from you and will not listen to anything you say (e.g. they really want your shoes). The child is asked what they should do if a little child argues with them and does not listen. Some children realise that it is best to ignore the three-year-old, whereas other children think that they should argue back. The child is asked to consider what would happen if they argue back, which can be investigated via role play. The therapist pretends to be a three-year-old toddler who wants the child's shoes. The child is asked to argue with this three-year-old as much as possible about not getting the shoes. Throughout the role play, the therapist always argues back with reasons why the child should give them their shoes. After a few minutes of arguing, the therapist asks the child questions to elicit the conclusion that arguing is unhelpful. These questions might include:

- What happened when you argued with me about the shoes?
- When you continued to argue with me, did the argument get bigger or smaller?
- What sort of things were you thinking about when you argued with me, thoughts about shoes or normal thoughts about life?

The child is then asked how arguing with a child might be similar to arguing with OCD (e.g. OCD always argues back, OCD doesn't care if you have good reasons, OCD just wants to win, OCD doesn't fight fair, the more you argue with the OCD the more OCD tries to scare you with other thoughts). Once the child realises that they cannot win an argument against OCD, the therapist can ask:

- If you can never win an argument with OCD, should you bother arguing at all?
- What should you do instead of arguing (e.g. ignore OCD as if he were a little child, and carry on with what you were doing before OCD interrupted you)?

Finding out what happens if you look out for harm

If a child engages in selective attention (e.g. looking for dirt, looking for things that are not symmetrical, focusing on bodily sensations for signs of harm), they should be helped to consider the impact of this unhelpful behaviour. The goal is for the child to realise that looking for danger is counterproductive because:

- it makes danger appear more common than it really is
- selectively focusing on the body can intensify physical sensations.

The unhelpfulness of 'looking for harm' can be illustrated by asking the child to look for harm related to OCD for a few minutes. For example, for fear of contamination, ask the child to look for dirt and germs. If the child is bothered by asymmetry, ask them to look for things that are uneven. If the child fears choking, then focus on swallowing. The therapist then asks the child what happened when they started to look for danger on purpose. Most children are able to report that they had lots of worrying thoughts, that they felt scared and that they noticed lots of scary things. Without prior warning, the therapist engages the child in an enjoyable game for a few minutes and then asks the child what happened to their thoughts and feelings about danger when they carried on with life and had some fun. Most children report that their thoughts and worry about harm disappeared. The child is then asked what made them feel better – looking for danger or carrying on with life. As soon the child understands that 'looking for danger' makes their belief about danger grow bigger and also triggers more worrying thoughts, the child is asked to draw an arrow from 'looking for harm' back to their 'beliefs' and 'intrusive thoughts' in bright red ink. The child is then asked to explain in their own words what this arrow means.

'Pushing it' experiments

As new healthy beliefs develop (e.g. rituals don't work, rituals make me worry more and it is okay to have intrusive thoughts), it is not uncommon for a child to display reluctance to push OCD any further. This reluctance may be due to a concern that OCD will come back if pushed too far. However, the child needs to go as far as possible in order to find out that OCD really is a liar. The therapist continues to explain that the only way to totally get rid of OCD is to do *'pushing it'* experiments. The child is told that there are three ways to deal with OCD:

- They can give in to OCD and make the problem worse
- They can not give in to OCD and make OCD smaller
- They can do 'pushing it' experiments and totally get rid of OCD.

For example, if the child has a fear of contamination the therapist could drop a pen on the ground and ask the child what they should do if they want to give into OCD (e.g. don't pick up the pen or wash their hands after picking up the pen). The child is then asked what they could do if they decide not to give in to OCD (e.g. pick up the pen normally and do not wash their hands). Lastly, the child is asked what they could do if they want to do a 'pushing it' experiment so that OCD is kicked out of their life (e.g. rub their hand all over the floor while picking up the pen and then wipe their hand over their face).

> 'Pushing it' experiments are helpful in working towards getting rid of the OCD completely.

Dealing with reassurance seeking

Many parents of younger children describe how they themselves become involved in the OCD as their child asks them for reassurance, e.g. that their intrusive thoughts will not come true. The cycle of reassurance seeking can be illustrated to the family and child using the itchy bite metaphor again. Reassurance seeking provides initial relief, but ends up making the problem worse because the child wants reassurance again, just as scratching relieves an itch initially but not in the longer term. Using the formulation of the problem, the therapist should guide the child to draw an arrow from 'reassurance' back to the 'belief' to show that reassurance ends up making the problem worse. The child is also asked what kind of thoughts they have when they ask for reassurance; that is, do they think about intrusive worries or do they think about everyday fun stuff? Most children acknowledge that asking for reassurance results in even more worrying thoughts and questions. Again, the child can show this on the diagram by drawing an arrow from 'reassurance' all the way to 'intrusive thoughts' in bright red ink.

Many parents report that they are at a loss with regard to how to manage their child's request for reassurance. Although the general aim is to help parents withdraw from providing reassurance, if this is done suddenly without the child's awareness it can lead to an increase in distress and oppositional behaviour. It is preferable to engage the child in designing a plan for managing reassurance seeking. It is best to begin this conversation after the child has a basic understanding of how reassurance works (i.e. it is like scratching an itchy bite and makes the problem worse). The therapist can then ask the child if they should continue asking for reassurance and if they think their parents should continue giving reassurance. As soon as the child agrees that reassurance needs to stop in order to beat OCD, the therapist asks the child what their parents could do to help them when they want reassurance. A list of possible ideas can be presented to the child and parent if they are unable to generate their own solutions, for example:

- play a game together
- watch a DVD
- talk about something else
- tell OCD that he is a big bully and to go away
- Mummy could remind you that this is OCD being a mean bully
- Mummy could say 'Let's do something else and ignore OCD'
- remind myself that Mummy is not being mean to me, but she is being mean to OCD.

It may be helpful if the child and therapist write out a plan on a sheet of paper using words and pictures. It can also be helpful to set up a score sheet for OCD and the child. The child receives a point if they do not ask for reassurance over a specified time, whereas OCD receives a point if he bullies the child into asking for reassurance. The child is encouraged to reflect on why they want to win more points (e.g. because reassurance is like feeding OCD and if you stop giving reassurance OCD will starve to death). As the child asks for reassurance less, the child and parent are encouraged to recognise that the problem lessens as reassurance declines.

> - If parents suddenly withdraw reassurance without the child's awareness, this can lead to an increase in distress and oppositional behaviour.
> - It is crucial that the child understands why reassurance can keep the problem going and helpful if they are engaged in designing a plan for managing reassurance.

Obstacles to treatment

If the child does not report thoughts or beliefs

It is common for many young children to report that they do not have intrusive thoughts. It may then be helpful to ask the child what would happen if they do not do their rituals, or if they do their rituals wrong. If the child is still unable to describe any intrusive thoughts, the therapist could say that it is perfectly normal to forget why we do things, especially if we have been doing things like rituals for a long time. This means that there is really a reason, but that we have forgotten what that reason is. The child might then be encouraged to view OCD as a mean horrible bully who makes the child do rituals without telling them why. Then the therapist and child consider the possibility that OCD's reasons for rituals might not be very good and might even be lies. Together, they work to discover OCD's reasons by refusing to do a ritual next time and then carefully listening for the reason OCD gives them. Even if OCD does not provide a good reason, this experiment is still helpful because the child may learn (a) that he or she does not have to do rituals and (b) that nothing bad happens.

Managing oppositional behaviour

Although parents are usually present in sessions, if a child becomes increasingly oppositional it may be helpful to see the child on their own for some of the time. One technique for managing oppositional behaviour involves asking the child if they are someone who likes to be bossed around all the time or if are they someone who likes to stand up for themselves. The aim is to build motivation for treatment by helping the child conclude that OCD is pushing them around too much and that they will not put up with this.

Relapse prevention

Setback planning for younger children involves family members as well as the child themselves. The therapist should describe the appearance of new habits as helping families to view relapse as an opportunity to practise beating OCD. Working together, the family and therapist prepare a plan so that they can react calmly. With younger children this plan can be summarised and presented in whatever format is most suitable for the child (e.g. as an OCD picture book, in poster format, on audio tape and video-recording, or colourful pamphlets). The plan should remind the child that they can respond to OCD in three ways:

• give in to OCD the bully
• not give in to OCD
• do experiments that make OCD disappear (e.g. doing 'pushing it' experiments).

A fun way to help the child plan is for the therapist to pretend to be OCD and try to trick the child with lots of lies (e.g. 'All germs are dangerous.' 'It is all your fault if something bad happens.' 'Rituals make you feel happy.'). The child is encouraged to tell OCD the real truth (e.g. 'Most germs are fine.' 'It is not my fault.' 'Rituals make me worry.').

Alternatively, treatment can be summarised by making a list of questions about OCD and attaching these questions to the back of photos of various children. The child is asked to pretend that they are on a talkback radio show for children with OCD. The child is asked to pick one photo at a time and to answer that child's question about OCD. An example of a typical question is as follows: 'Hello, my name is Emily and I have scary thoughts that my mother will die. Is this normal?' At the end of treatment, it can be helpful to offer the family two or three booster sessions and encourage them to contact the therapist if they require further support.

- Setback planning should involve family members as well as the child themselves.
- The plan should be summarised and presented in a suitable format for the child, such as on video-tape or as a picture book.
- Games and role plays can be fun and helpful in consolidating what has been learnt.

6

CBT with adolescents

Polly Waite

The nature of adolescence

Adolescence characterises the period between childhood and adulthood, as young people go through a number of changes physically and mentally and become more independent. As puberty occurs earlier and with more young people going into higher education, this period can span up to a decade, which can make generalisations difficult.

As youngsters move through adolescence, cognitive skills develop and there is a shift towards more abstract thinking and a greater ability for logical and scientific reasoning (Coleman and Hendry, 1999). Skills develop so that adolescents are better able to generate hypotheses and explanations about concrete events. Abilities such as problem solving improve as they are able to suggest alternative hypotheses, test them out against facts and then disregard hypotheses that prove to be wrong. They are more able to stand back and think about their own thinking processes as well of those of other people.

For many years, adolescence has been considered to be a transitional period. This transition can be positive and may involve looking forward to the future and the freedom and opportunities it brings, such as leaving school, establishing greater independence from the family or developing relationships. However, it can also bring feelings of anxiety about the future, in adjusting to new roles with family, friends and others and developing a sense of identity. Psychological problems can interfere with the young person's progress through adolescence, e.g. becoming more independent, getting through school and developing relationships.

CBT with adolescents

Given that developing autonomy and independence is one of the key tasks for adolescents, it is important that therapy gives the young person experience of achieving control over their life. To begin with, this may consist of making decisions around whether and how family members are involved in therapy. As therapy progresses, the young person will be encouraged to develop goals that guide the direction and pace of therapy. This is often a time where family members (and therapists) may also have ideas about what goals may be helpful and make a difference. However, these may not always be the same goals as the young person's and therefore it is important that it is the young person's goals that remain primary. As with younger children, parents and family members may often have requested treatment so for the young person to engage in therapy and feel motivated to change, it is essential that they are making choices and working towards goals that will make a difference to them.

The same principles apply when it comes to planning and carrying out behavioural experiments. As therapists, we often have ideas about what may be a good first step and yet discussion with the young person may reveal this to be out of line with where they want to begin. It is essential that the young person does not feel under pressure to carry things out that they do not want to do and, when possible, that they take the lead in planning experiments. However, there may be times when working on the adolescent's agenda may result in them struggling to make progress. If this is the case, it can be helpful to revisit the young person's goals. In most cases, they will have specified getting rid of the OCD as a medium to long-term goal and so it can be helpful to think through whether they are currently on track to achieve it and if not, what they would need to do differently to get there.

> Therapy needs to give the young person experience of achieving control over their life and to facilitate adolescent tasks of developing autonomy and independence.

Role of the family in treatment

When carrying out therapy with young people, the therapist must take into account that they are unlikely to have separated entirely from their parents or family during adolescence. Factors such as the circumstances of the family, ethnicity and culture will affect the degree to which the young person maintains their ties with their family as they move into adulthood. In general, there is evidence that a continuing connectedness with parents is helpful (Grotevant and Cooper, 1986), in a relationship that involves warmth, structure, a support for autonomy and good communication (Coleman and Hendry, 1999). Consequently, it is the role of the therapist to facilitate this, while also respecting the choices the young person makes about family involvement.

In general, the young person will decide whether or not they would like family members to attend sessions and typically as adolescents get older they may prefer to have sessions on their own with the therapist. Sometimes family members may have very little involvement in therapy and this can work well. However, there may be other occasions where a lack of involvement can be detrimental, e.g. if a parent continues to provide reassurance to the young person and this impedes the progress of therapy. Thinking about the involvement of family members should always be guided by the individual case formulation. If the therapist has reason to think that it may be helpful for the family to be involved, they may need to work out with the young person how they can achieve this. This could include having a parent in the room for the last ten minutes of a session so that the young person can convey any important information, having separate sessions with family members or the therapist speaking to family members over the telephone. Equally, there may be times when the family is attending sessions and the therapist feels that it may be helpful to have sessions on their own with the young person, e.g. if the young person needs to develop autonomy or if the presence of family members leads to conflict. This is covered in more detail in Chapter 7.

It is also critical that the therapist considers the role of the family in identifying predisposing, precipitating and maintaining factors that relate to the problem. For example, the young person may be given little responsibility within the family and the therapist may hypothesise that this may be contributing to the development and maintenance of the OCD. There may be certain standards or rules around cleanliness and hygiene or moral conduct that may be relevant and if not addressed may lead to problems in treatment. It is crucial that the therapist finds a way to incorporate this in therapy, either informally through discussion or, when necessary, more formally in a written formulation. This is covered in detail in Chapter 7 and consequently the focus of this chapter will be on how to work with the young person individually.

- The role of the therapist is to facilitate continuing connectedness with parents while respecting the choices the young person makes about family involvement.
- While the therapist is working primarily with the young person, they will need to address any systemic factors that may be maintaining the problem.

Beginning to make sense of the problem

As outlined in Chapter 4, therapy starts with the development of a formulation that the therapist and young person use to make sense of the problem. This is carried out in a collaborative way by using recent examples and focuses in at the problem level and maintenance cycles. As mentioned earlier, this does not typically include family factors or experiences that may have led to the development of the problem, although the therapist will have considered these and will aim to address relevant factors in therapy. The formulation is normally put together as a diagram. While younger children may prefer to be able to draw it out themselves and add pictures, this can feel embarrassing for adolescents and so many prefer for this to be done by the therapist.

> Jacob was a 13-year-old who came to treatment after his mum became deeply concerned about him. This followed an incident on holiday where Jacob was in a public toilet and a young boy came into the toilets on his own. Jacob described having had a thought about having molested this boy and later on, as he went over the thought in his mind, he began to be concerned that he may have carried out the thought without being aware of it. The more he tried to argue with the thought, the more concerned he became that he may have 'lost control'. Following this, he began to believe that he was a paedophile and took what he described as safety measures to stop him acting on his thoughts. This included avoiding situations where there may be young children, such as parks and playgrounds, keeping his hands in his pockets and crossing over the road if he was about to walk past a child. He worried that if he were to hear or read about any murderers, that by thinking about them or looking at their pictures he could turn into that person. He also described feeling that he may say something bad without knowing. Consequently, he found it difficult to write text messages or cards to friends as he worried that he may write an insult without being aware of it and would check what he had written over and over again. Finally, he described feeling that if he ever said anything bad about anyone, this meant he was a bad person.

Figure 6.1 shows Jacob's formulation. He had already noticed that he had spent a lot of time thinking the thought through afterwards and that this was because he wanted to feel certain about what had happened in the toilet. However, he was also aware that the more time he spent thinking about the thought and what it meant to him, the less certain he became. The therapist was able to use this to show how it acted as a vicious cycle, in that the more he thought about it, the more he kept the worry going. Jacob identified that the other behaviours worked in the same way and that being on the lookout and checking also kept him believing that he may have harmed the boy.

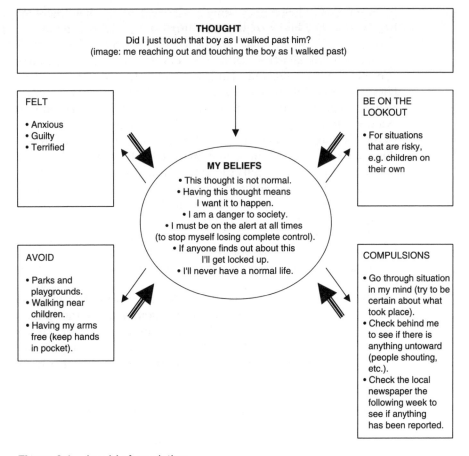

Figure 6.1 Jacob's formulation

Normalising intrusive thoughts

One of the key tasks in CBT is for the young person to come to the realisation that most people have intrusive thoughts. It can be interesting to ask the young person (and family members) to guess what percentage of people has intrusive thoughts. In most cases, people significantly underestimate the proportion, believing that it is the obsessional thought itself that is the problem in OCD. Research (e.g. Rachman and Hodgson, 1980) and personal examples can be helpful to support the point. This is particularly important in a case like Jacob's, where many of his thoughts are around harming others and have led him to conclude that this means he is a bad and potentially dangerous person, with associated feelings of fear, guilt and shame.

As well as the therapist giving examples of thoughts that they and other people commonly have, it can be helpful to ask family members to share any examples of thoughts they have experienced. Often parents recollect having had thoughts of loved ones being in an accident or when their children were babies that they had stopped breathing (and perhaps gone in to check that they were still alive). When parents recall intrusive thoughts of harming others, they frequently recall thoughts of harming their children either accidentally (e.g. dropping them) or intentionally (e.g. smothering them, particularly when the child was a baby and cried a lot). Sometimes, family members cannot recall any intrusive thoughts and so it is often helpful to begin with examples to prompt their memories. When family members initially cannot recall any thoughts but then identify with examples provided by the therapist, this can be used to illustrate that it was not that they did not have thoughts, it is just that they were not seen as being meaningful and therefore they paid little attention to them, which helps to reinforce the formulation of the problem.

Once the young person accepts that most people experience intrusive thoughts, the aim is for them to reach an understanding that it is the meaning they attach to it that causes the distress and leads to compulsions. One way to achieve this with young people is to consider a scenario and think about how two different people might react, for example:

Therapist: Let's think about a situation involving two girls, Jessica and Charlotte. They are both standing on a train platform waiting for a train and they are standing right at the edge of the platform. Suddenly, out of the blue, they have a thought about throwing themselves off the platform in front of the train. Jessica does not have OCD so what do you think happens when she gets the thought?

Jacob: She ignores it, doesn't think it's a big deal.

Therapist: What do you think she does?

Jacob: Nothing probably.

Therapist: That's right. She carries on standing and waits for the train, which then pulls into the station. Let's now take Charlotte. She has exactly the same thought but she has OCD. What do you think she makes of it?

Jacob: She might know that she wouldn't really do it, but might still be scared in case she might do it, in case she just loses control.

Therapist: Right, so if she thinks that, what do you think she might do?

Jacob: She might move away from the edge of the platform and only walk to the edge when the train is there and she feels safe or she might ask someone like her mum whether she is okay.

Therapist: So what is different about these two girls?

Jacob: What they do. Jessica ignores the thought and carries on, but Charlotte is worried and so she moves away from the edge.

Therapist: What is it that makes them act so differently?

Jacob: It's what they think the thought means. Jessica thinks it doesn't mean anything, but Charlotte thinks it means that she might lose control.

This scenario can also be used to demonstrate the maintenance cycle of OCD, as the young person is encouraged to think about how the two girls might behave in the future. For example, Jessica is likely to carry on standing at the edge of the platform and not be bothered by the thought if it pops into her mind again, whereas Charlotte may ask for further reassurance, stop catching trains or putting herself in other situations where she feels she may lose control. As she does more to try to stop herself losing control, this will have the effect of making her believe more and more that she may lose control if she does not do these things.

It can also be helpful to ask the young person which of these girls is likely to have more of these intrusive thoughts and why that might be, to illustrate that as Charlotte carries out more and more compulsions or 'safety' strategies, intrusive thoughts become more frequent and more intense. Finally, it can be helpful to then turn to look at how the problem is working for the young person themselves and whether it may be working in the same way.

- Therapy starts with the development of a formulation that the therapist and young person use to be able to make sense of the problem.

- This is carried out in a collaborative way by using recent examples and focuses in at the problem level and maintenance cycles.

- Once the young person accepts that most people experience intrusive thoughts, the aim is for them to reach an understanding that it is the meaning that they attach to it that causes the distress and leads to compulsions.

Goal setting

In general, the aim of goals is to identify what the person wants to change, guide plans for change and provide guideposts to track progress. With adolescents in particular, it is worth spending time on long-term goals and this is often the best place to start. By the time some young people reach their teenage years they may have had OCD for a long time and may also have received previous treatment. Consequently, it is not uncommon for some young people (and their families) to already hold beliefs about their OCD being untreatable and some will already have adjusted their expectations accordingly. It is crucial that the therapist encourages the young person to think about getting rid of the OCD, not just moderating or learning to live with it. Often young people and their families are surprised to learn that OCD is treatable and have not even dared hope that there might be a day when the young person no longer has to worry when they get intrusive thoughts or carry out time-consuming compulsions. It is the role of the therapist to engender hope and encourage the young person to think about their dreams for the future and how life might be without OCD. It is these dreams, in the form of long-term goals, that the young person and therapist return to when treatment is scary and difficult and this can enable the young person to keep going.

Goals are most helpful when they are specific and measurable and set within definite timeframes, such as the next week, two weeks or months. The following questions can be helpful to identify goals and break them down:

- How would things be different?
- How would someone else know if you had reached this goal?
- What are the steps you would need to take to reach your long-term goal?
- How would you know if you were half-way there?
- What would you need to do for things to be 1 per cent better?
- If your friend had this as a goal, what would you advise them to do to begin to work towards it?

> Ellie was a 16-year-old who had a fear of germs. This began gradually around three years ago, after her dad died unexpectedly of a heart attack. She worried about becoming contaminated through contact with germs, through touching door handles, light switches, objects in the bathroom and her brother's hamster. School felt especially contaminated and as a result she would shower excessively when arriving home from school and insist on keeping her school uniform, bag, folders and books in the spare room. Her worry was about spreading germs to her mum, nan and two younger brothers. She was concerned that this could cause them to become ill, with symptoms including vomiting, diarrhoea, a raised temperature and coughing or sneezing, which in the worse possible scenario could lead them to die. She avoided touching anything she worried was contaminated and so would open doors with her foot, use tissues to touch objects and found it difficult to prepare food or drinks for other people.

Ellie's goals are shown in Figure 6.2. By starting with long-term goals, she was able to see that she needed to be able to get rid of the OCD in order to live the kind of life she wanted. This made it easier to identify medium-term and short-term goals. Not all the goals are directly related to getting rid of the OCD and some are around re-establishing normal activities and starting to do the things she has been avoiding. Short-term goals are regularly reviewed and further goals are developed as therapy progresses.

> Goals that are set by the young person are essential in order to help with motivation and it is crucial that they are regularly reviewed and that sessions are clearly related to goals.

Long-term goals

- Do GCSEs.
- Go to the end of school prom.
- Train and get a job as a veterinary nurse.
- Learn to drive.
- Have a boyfriend.
- Move out of home.
- Get married.
- Have children.

Medium-term goals

- Get rid of the OCD!
- Sleep over at friends' houses.
- Use the computer for coursework.
- Store school stuff in my bedroom.
- Go Christmas shopping with Mum.

Short-term goals

- Ignore thoughts – tell myself it's just a stupid thought and then distract myself with something else.
- Find out about reassurance – try experiment to see if it really makes my worry worse or better (ten minutes asking Mum if she is okay loads and then ten minutes not asking at all – record results).
- Make Nan a cup of tea.
- Touch door handle with my hand and not wash my hands afterwards.

Figure 6.2   Ellie's goals

Building an alternative view of the problem

Early on in therapy, it is helpful to externalise the OCD and to set up two opposing ways of making sense of how the world works. As with younger children, this helps the young person to step outside the beliefs and be able to think about them in a more objective way. With adolescents too it is extremely helpful to phrase questions in a way that allows them and their families to see OCD as separate to them, e.g. 'What does OCD tell you would happen if you did not do a compulsion?'

When building up an alternative way of understanding how the world works, the therapist and young person write out the two contrasting explanations about OCD that can be tested through experiments. On one side is the OCD and on the other side is the opposite of OCD and the specific predictions on each side will be related to the individual's idiosyncratic beliefs. While younger children often enjoy developing and drawing out characters to represent these two explanations, adolescents often choose to call them

OCD predicts	Opposite of OCD predicts
If I don't do a habit: • People I love could get ill and even die. • It's my responsibility to stop this happening and if I don't do a habit and this happens it would be my fault. • I will keep on worrying about it and won't be able to concentrate on anything else.	*If I don't do a habit:* • It won't make a difference – habits don't work. • If people get ill, it is just a coincidence – everyone gets ill from time to time. • Because what I do doesn't make a difference, then it is not my responsibility. • I might worry to begin with, but after a while I will forget about it.

Figure 6.3   Ellie's predictions about what will happen if she does not neutralise after having an obsessional thought

'OCD' and something like, 'the opposite of OCD' or 'not OCD'. Figure 6.3 shows Ellie's explanations of what OCD tells her and an alternative way of understanding how the world may work.

> • It is helpful to externalise the OCD to help the young person step outside the beliefs and see them in a more objective way.
>
> • The therapist and young person develop two opposing ways of making sense of how the world works (an OCD explanation and a competing explanation) and these are used to guide discussion and behavioural experiments.

Behavioural experiments

As described in previous chapters, the purpose of behavioural experiments is to help the young person build up a body of evidence to support a new way of thinking about their problem (i.e. that they worry too much about danger), while decreasing evidence for their previously held interpretation of the problem (i.e. that they are in danger). As much as possible, the young person needs to be involved in designing experiments and it is crucial that they are always clear about the rationale for the experiment and before carrying it out have made predictions about what they believe will happen and what this would mean.

With all behavioural experiments, it is important to spend time afterwards exploring what happened through guided discovery. This includes finding out what the young person made of what happened and what it told them about how the world works generally:

- How does it fit in with the young person's original prediction?
- Was the original prediction correct or incorrect?
- Does this fit best with the idea that the problem is about danger or does it fit better with the idea that the problem is about worry?
- How does this experiment relate to the formulation of the young person's problem?
- How can this new understanding be carried forward in real life and further experiments?

It is worth taking time to reflect on experiments and to relate it back to the young person's assumptions and beliefs in order for them to generalise what they have learned. By focusing on how the results of the experiment relate to the bigger picture, this also helps to ensure that the experiment does not end up as a form of reassurance.

> Behavioural experiments need to have a clear rationale. Before carrying out an experiment, the young person needs to think about what they would predict will happen. After the experiment is carried out, it is important to reflect on the outcome and relate it back to the young person's assumptions and beliefs in order for them to generalise what they have learned.

When carrying out behavioural experiments, it is also important to be aware that the therapist or other people's presence or involvement may have the effect of reducing how the young person sees their personal responsibility. As a result, the young person may feel less anxious and less likely to feel that harm could occur. In general, it is helpful for the young person to become more responsible for experiments through the course of therapy. This includes designing them and carrying them out increasingly independently. This also has the added benefit of facilitating the young person's autonomy and self-confidence. With adolescents in particular, it can be helpful to have a discussion about the role of parents and other family members when carrying out experiments between sessions. Although parents are often keen to help and be involved, young people often prefer to carry out experiments independently and report back to the therapist and family in the following session. It is helpful to think this through with the young person early on so that everyone is clear about their role.

Tom was a 14-year-old who developed OCD after being bullied at school. This began at the start of secondary school, when he was ostracised by a group of friends and bullied verbally. As a result, he moved to another class and his teachers then noticed a number of 'odd' behaviours, such as him hovering near doorways, going in and out of doorways more than once and repeating other actions. Although he was able to establish a new group of friends, over time these behaviours increased and by the time he was referred to the clinic he was spending more than ten hours a day doing compulsions. His obsessional thoughts were mainly around the worry that he would be bullied again, thinking of the people who bullied him, the worry he would lose his friends or that other 'bad luck' might happen to him, such as doing badly in a test or getting a detention. He continued to have problems with repeating (written work if it did not 'feel right', walking through doors, up and down stairs, getting up and down from a chair, in and out of the shower) and would do actions holding a 'good' thought a certain number of times. 'Good' thoughts were thoughts of his friends, things they had enjoyed doing together and happy memories with his family.

Changing beliefs about thoughts

Thought–action fusion, the idea that thinking a thought can increase the chance of the thought coming true, is prevalent in OCD. In Tom's case, he believed that thinking about the group who bullied him could lead to him being bullied again. His therapist asked him to rate how strongly he held this belief and he rated it as 95 per cent. However, when asked about the mechanism through which this occurred, Tom was unclear. He did not feel that he had any special powers and struggled to account for how it may happen. However, he was able to describe how he felt that if he were to have a thought and not neutralise then bad luck would happen to him within the next day or so.

Tom and his therapist planned some experiments to investigate this further. They began with an experiment that would not lead to actual harm so that Tom could see what would happen in a less 'risky' way and then experiments became increasingly more 'risky'. These experiments are illustrated in Figure 6.4. To begin with they designed the experiments so they would be able to find out the results straightaway. The therapist modelled more difficult experiments first to encourage Tom to do experiments himself. Whilst doing the experiments, Tom and the therapist had a discussion which covered the following:

- The importance of Tom rating his predictions based on his feeling deep down rather than what he knew logically should happen.
- That if they did come true, the mechanism through which this would happen, i.e. did he feel he had any special powers? If not, how would it work?
- Could he kill things (like snakes – which his mum was scared of) by thinking about it?
- Could he make good things happen (for example, winning the lottery) as well as bad things – and if not, why not?
- Did he notice any relationship between how worried he was and how likely he felt it was that something bad would happen?
- Did this fit in more with the idea that this is really dangerous (OCD) or that he was worrying too much about it being dangerous (the opposite of OCD)?

Over the following week, both Tom and the therapist continued with

Thinking experiments – week 1	How worried am I? (0–10)	Chance of it happening? (0–100%)	Did it happen?
Thinking of someone knocking on door and then walking in.	0	5	No
Therapist thinking of me falling over as I walk up and down the corridor.	2	20	No
Thinking of the therapist tripping and falling over while she is out of the room walking down the stairs.	2	15	No
The therapist thinking of the receptionist having a heart attack.	7	60	No
Me thinking of the receptionist having a heart attack.	7	60	No
Therapist thinking of me having a heart attack.	6	50	No
Me thinking of my Mum having a heart attack.	8	80	No
Me and therapist thinking about people who have committed murder would lead to bad luck for us the next day.	9	85	Report back next week

Figure 6.4 Tom's thinking experiments

thinking experiments to see if either or them could make good or bad things happen. By the following week, Tom decided to try to put the thought of the bullies into his head without doing a mental ritual afterwards, to test out his original belief that thinking about them would cause something bad to happen the following day. By repeating these experiments a number of times, this allowed him to develop a less threatening interpretation, which was that thoughts were actually not that important, but he had been worrying too much about it.

Estimating threat

One of the central beliefs in OCD is around the overestimation of threat, in that the estimation of the probability and/or severity of harm is exaggerated. Theoretically, threat estimation (and inflated responsibility) is most strongly linked to thoughts of contamination and harming others (OCCWG, 2001; Salkovskis, 1985).

Once Ellie and her therapist developed an understanding of her problem around germs, Ellie was encouraged to think about whether the problem fitted more with the idea that the world is dangerous or with the idea that she is worrying too much about the world being dangerous. So far she had been thinking about the problem as being around germs and so her therapist carried out a behavioural experiment to start to test out what the problem was really about. Ellie was asked what she thought would happen if the therapist licked the bottom of her shoe. Ellie predicted that there was a 90 per cent chance that the therapist would get a stomach bug as she could have trodden in dirt, mud or dog mess. The therapist then licked the bottom of her shoe so that Ellie could see and the following week reported back the results of the experiment. The following session, the therapist suggested that she do another over-the-top experiment again to learn more about how Ellie had been estimating the likelihood of harm. She and Ellie went into the bathroom and the therapist touched the objects that Ellie felt were con- taminated, such as the taps, toilet flush and seat and then licked her hands afterwards. Prior to this, the therapist made sure that Ellie was clear about the purpose of this experiment and got her to make some predictions that they could test out. By modelling more extreme experiments, this allowed Ellie to see that the therapist was willing to take risks and also that she herself could cope with the anxiety this entailed. It also meant that she felt more willing to carry out some experiments herself.

Ellie found it helpful to find out that she had been overestimating the likelihood of harm in experiments carried out by the therapist. She described how this had led her to feel in her head that germs were not as dangerous as she had thought, but in her heart she still felt that if she were to touch something she (and then other people) would get ill. She felt that the next step would be to find out what would happen if she were to touch something she felt was germy and then not do a compulsion. She and the therapist came up with an experiment where she touched a door handle and then immediately ate a sweet without washing her hands first (see Figure 6.5). The results of this experiment enabled her to see that it worked in the same way as the therapist's more extreme experiments and that the problem appeared to be more related to worry than actual harm.

Dealing with uncertainty and perfectionism

The belief that it is necessary to be certain and that it will be impossible to cope without complete certainty can be a problem in OCD. In particular, young people with checking compulsions often describe the aim as being to achieve certainty. Behavioural experiments can be helpful to test this out. One of Jacob's worries was around the idea that if he did not check text messages before he sent them, he may have written an insult without realis- ing. As a result, he checked text messages again and again before sending them. He and his therapist carried out an experiment to see if checking led to greater certainty. They designed an experiment where he wrote a text to his friend and then behaved in a completely OCD way by checking it

Thought to test out	Experiment	What do I predict will happen?	What happened?	What does this mean?	What does this mean about how the world really works?
That touching something I think is germy will make me ill.	Touch door handle and then eat a sweet without washing my hands first.	That there is an 80% chance I will get a stomach bug (which I could pass on) and that I will feel really worried and not be able to forget about it.	I touched it and didn't wash my hands. I didn't get ill and nor did anyone else and after a while I forgot about the experiment. Later on, I felt really pleased.	That OCD is lying. It worked more in the opposite way.	This fitted in better with the idea that the problem is about worry, rather than the problem is about germs making people ill.

Figure 6.5 Ellie's experiment

multiple times. He then wrote another text and then did the opposite of what OCD would tell him to do, by sending it without checking it first. He predicted that on the second occasion, he would feel more uncertain and worried about it. Interestingly, after checking each text he felt uncertain and was worried that by pressing the keys on his mobile phone to check it he may actually be changing the text. He also learned that he was actually more certain when he did not check the text and soon after sending it he actually forgot about it. The following week, he reported back that he had spoken to the friend that evening and felt confident that although he had not checked the second text, this had not caused him to insult his friend. As a result he concluded that this experiment fitted in more with the idea that the problem was about worrying too much rather than the risk of something bad happening.

> Experiments are essential in exploring beliefs around thought–action fusion, threat estimation and dealing with uncertainty and perfectionism.

Discussion techniques

Changing beliefs about personal responsibility

An exaggerated belief by the young person that they have the power to bring about or prevent bad things happening is common in OCD. This results in feeling obliged to take every possible action to make sure the bad thing does not happen or to make sure that nothing they have done or not done could have a negative impact. Discussion and techniques, such as pie charts, can be useful in modifying the young person's negative beliefs. In particular, the aim is for the young person to find out that they tend to overestimate their personal responsibility in relation to their obsessions and to learn that it is difficult to partition overall responsibility because of many interacting contributory factors.

This technique was used with Ellie to explore her belief that she was 90 per cent responsible for causing her father's heart attack. To begin with, she was asked to make a list of all the things that may have contributed to him dying, however slight. She began with her belief that she had caused his heart attack by thinking about him dying some weeks before the event. She then identified all the other factors that may have been involved:

1   Her thinking of her dad dying.
2   Smoking.
3   In his genes.
4   High blood pressure.
5   Not doing enough exercise.
6   Diet.
7   Being overweight.

Once she generated all these different factors, the therapist asked her to identify how much she believed each one contributed. As she went through this process, the therapist drew a pie chart and divided it up according to Ellie's ratings. By beginning at the bottom of the list and ending with her own involvement, she was able to see it in relation to other significant factors (see Figure 6.6).

When the therapist asked Ellie what she made of this, she described being surprised that her thinking about her father dying had been such a small amount. When she considered it in the context of all the other factors, she felt it was insignificant. This, in conjunction with the evidence she had collected through other behavioural experiments, reduced her belief in her responsibility for her father's death.

Dealing with uncertainty and perfectionism

It can be useful to use surveys to find out about other people's feelings of certainty, e.g. asking people to rate as a percentage how certain they are that they locked their house that morning, closed and locked all the windows or did not make any mistakes at school or work. The young person can be asked to recall occasions in the past where certainty was not achieved and they had to live with doubt, such as waiting for exam results. Were they able to cope with this and get on with life? Using Socratic questioning, it can be helpful to think about how life would be if you were only able to do things

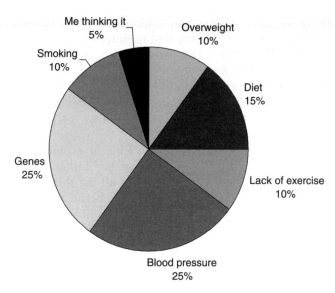

Figure 6.6 Ellie's responsibility pie chart

that you knew were certain and risk free or to consider the pros and cons of tolerating uncertainty.

As with trying to achieve certainty, there may also be beliefs around needing to be perfect. This involves the idea that there is a perfect solution to every problem, that doing something perfectly is not only possible but also necessary, and that even minor mistakes will have serious consequences. In this case, the aim is for the young person to find out that there are disadvantages in being perfect, that perfection is rarely achieved and mistakes are normal and do not result in serious negative consequences and to develop alternative ways of thinking that are not so 'all or nothing'.

Jacob was encouraged to think about this through the use of a continuum (see Figure 6.7). After drawing it out and providing labels for each end, he then identified a number of people, such as family and friends and public figures (including people that he thought were really good and really bad, e.g. the Dalai Lama and Hitler) and placed them on the continuum. Finally, he put himself on it. This enabled him to see that people were all over the line, but that most people fell somewhere around the middle. He then thought about his friend Joe, who was someone he thought was a good role model for how he wanted to be. When he came to place Joe on the line, he realised that he was about three quarters of the way along and not at the very end. This told him that you do not need to be perfect all the time to be a good person.

> Techniques such as pie charts or using continuums can be helpful in exploring and challenging beliefs around personal responsibility and the desire to be certain or perfect.

100% imperfect and evil
- Fails at everything
- Makes mistakes all the time
- Upsets everyone they meet
- Murders people
- Complains all the time
- Always rude and loses temper

100% perfect
- Does everything perfectly
- Never ever makes a mistake
- Never upsets anyone
- Helps other people all the time
- Never complains about anything
- Never rude/never loses temper

Figure 6.7 Jacob's continuum

Dealing with difficulties

Motivation

As acknowledged already, the request for help may not have actually been initiated by the young person and consequently they may feel ambivalent about change. This may not arise until some way into treatment as often this ambivalence is not expressed by the young person, but may be recognised through difficulty completing tasks inside or outside sessions. It is crucial that goals are identified early on and to be able to make links between having the OCD and whether the goals could still be achieved, particularly long-term goals such as finishing education, getting a job or moving out of home.

The process of identifying the pros and cons of staying the same and then the pros and cons of changing can be extremely helpful. When doing this, it is important that these are generated by the young person themselves rather than family. Typically there are more pros than cons to changing and many of the cons can be seen as speculative, in that they are what OCD tries to convince you rather than reality. If the young person is unsure about this, it could be helpful to suggest finding this out through experiments, rather than believing it without any evidence. If it turns out that the OCD is right, the therapist can then promise to help the young person to become obsessional again.

If the young person is quiet and unforthcoming

If the young person is quiet and unforthcoming in sessions, it is crucial to take a step back and explore what is going on rather than follow the session agenda. Clearly there may be a number of reasons for this:

- Is the young person having trouble understanding the content of the sessions?
- Are they feeling negative or overwhelmed and having trouble believing that therapy could help them?
- Are family members monopolising sessions and making it difficult for them to speak?
- Do they feel uncomfortable with the therapist?

Some adolescents will be less verbally articulate than others and may find some of the concepts more difficult to understand. If this is the case, it is essential that the therapist makes adaptations to the therapy. The therapist may need to go slower, regularly check the young person's understanding, get them to summarise what they have learnt more often and place more emphasis on metaphors, role plays and behavioural experiments. Some young people find therapy sessions awkward as they are with an unfamiliar adult talking about things that may be very uncomfortable. Therapists need to ensure that they are approachable, adapt their language and listen carefully to what the young person says. However, they may also need to keep sessions short, maximise the use of homework between sessions (perhaps with a parent or friend to help) and use written materials as an adjunct where possible.

Carrying out behavioural experiments

Before carrying out behavioural experiments, it is important to check that the young person understands the rationale for doing it and that they feel it would be helpful to carry out the experiment. Questions such as 'What would be the reason for doing this?' are important and if the young person is not clear about why the experiment is being carried out, it is important to consider the rationale with them. The risk of not doing this is that they may feel bullied into it and disengage from treatment and this can easily happen when therapists feel under time pressure and unintentionally become too didactic. It is always important to set up experiments so that the young person can say no and that the therapist responds to this without pressuring them. Control can be an important issue to consider when understanding a young person's reluctance to carry out an experiment and it is crucial that the young person feels they are in charge of what they do.

When designing behavioural experiments, it is often the case that compulsions cannot be easily replicated in the clinic room or when the triggers are not available. In most cases, home visits are of enormous value in understanding the problem and creating opportunities that are more 'real life' and more easily generalised to outside sessions.

The nature of behavioural experiments means that anything can happen and as a consequence sometimes results may initially appear to support OCD. For example, in experiments designed to test out the idea of whether thinking something can make it happen, there are occasions where the thought may come true. If the thought is about something that is not that unlikely to happen, such as the young person's younger brother falling over and hurting themselves, it can be helpful to consider this when planning the experiment. If he falls over now and again, how much would he have to fall over for it to be out of the ordinary, or could the prediction be more specific (e.g. he will fall over as soon as I've thought it and he will twist his left ankle and bang his right elbow)? Discussing the idea of coincidence beforehand can often be helpful and allows the young person to be able to deal with the various possible outcomes.

Completely eradicating the OCD

Most young people want to get rid of the OCD completely and state this as their medium or long-term goal. Although they will still experience intrusive thoughts (as do most of the population), they can dismiss them because they will not be interpreted in a meaningful way. Commonly in OCD, the young person will make progress and get around 70 per cent of the way towards eradicating the OCD and then struggle to go further. It is important to be able to normalise this experience, consider what may be going on and think about whether it is necessary to work towards completely getting rid of it. Analogies can be helpful, such as getting rid of weeds in the garden and thinking about how if you just pull out the weed without getting out the roots it grows back. Often the OCD has crept in and got worse over time and many young people recognise that this is what has happened in the past and that there is a danger that this would happen again.

It is helpful then to consider how it is possible to completely get rid of OCD and whether it works the same or differently to what they have already done. This was an issue that cropped up with Ellie:

Therapist: One of the things you mentioned last time is feeling that you are not strong enough to get to your final goal of getting rid of the OCD.

Ellie: Yes, I think generally I am coping quite well and I'm able to do stuff that is not so hard, but I'm not sure I will ever be able to completely get rid of it.

Therapist: You know when we did some of that stuff that was not so hard? If you cast your mind back to before we did it, did you feel that was going to be not hard or at the time did you think it would be hard?

Ellie: I thought it would be really hard.

Therapist: That's interesting. Are there other times recently when you've done things that are really hard?

Ellie: Started a new school.

Therapist: Yes, how did you manage to do that?

Ellie: I thought about when I had done it before and thought if I can do that I can do it again.

Therapist: So what does that suggest?

Ellie: I can do stuff that is scary.

Therapist: So what does that mean for what you might go on to do?

Ellie: I could think about the things I've already done to power me. I can go on to do things that I think will be hard.

Therapist: So bringing it back to our session today, what do you think would be good to do?

Ellie: I don't know.

Therapist: Is that 'I don't know' or 'I kind of know but what I'm thinking is too scary'?

Ellie:	Well, I know that I need to touch my school stuff but I don't want to do it.
Therapist:	If you think about your friend Catrina and if she was in a situation like this, what advice would you give her?
Ellie:	To push herself as far as she could but still be comfortable with the situation.
Therapist:	That sounds like really good advice. So if you were giving that advice to yourself what would you do in this session that would mean that you pushed yourself but still felt comfortable?
Ellie:	I don't know.
Therapist:	Well, we know from before that it is really important that you feel in control and that you are the one making the decision. So let's take a bit of time now and I'd like you to think about what we could do so that you feel you are pushing yourself but still feel comfortable.
Ellie:	I could touch my history folder and not wash my hands.
Therapist:	Okay, let's go and do it. You are in charge and you tell us what to do. Before we do it though, what do you predict will happen?

As with Ellie, in most cases, it is about the young person realising that they just need to carry on with what they have been doing and if they keep going they will eventually get there.

> Difficulties can arise when the young person is not sure whether change is worth it, if they do not understand the rationale for experiments, if they feel pressurised to do experiments and if they do not feel in control. If this occurs, it is crucial to step back and address this before moving on.

7

Working with families
Blake Stobie

Introduction

The involvement of family members and significant others in OCD is a common phenomenon. Family members may become involved in providing reassurance and assisting with the completion of compulsive rituals – sometimes to the extent that they may spend significantly more time ritualising than the young person. Alternatively, family members may refuse to participate in rituals and provide reassurance. With either response, the family system is likely to experience increased tension and conflict, as well as disruption to the goals and functioning of individual family members within their life cycle stages. In recognition of this, many clinicians advocate the explicit involvement of family members in therapy sessions where the individual case formulation suggests that the involvement of family members may be beneficial.

> - Family members are often involved in OCD, through the provision of reassurance and assisting with rituals; they are likely to experience tension, conflict and disruption.
> - Clinicians may use the formulation to determine whether involving family members in treatment may be appropriate in these instances.

Issues confronting therapists

Cognitive behavioural and family systems therapy approaches to the treatment of OCD are not easily reconciled. These two approaches can differ fundamentally on core issues of aetiology, therapist role, focus on symptomatology, means of intervention – even before considering the fact that many different schools of family therapy exist. The CBT approach has the advantage of being an empirically validated, focused approach with explicit models which describe how individuals develop and maintain anxiety-based problems. A key advantage of the CBT approach is its focus on the specific problem. On the other hand, whilst good CBT normalises problems and emphasises the importance of working collaboratively, systemic therapy approaches may consider broader contextual issues involved in maintaining and overcoming the problem, rather than focusing predominantly on the young person. Family and systemic therapies also have well-developed techniques for including family members within therapy sessions.

Strapping CBT techniques on to a family therapy intervention for OCD runs the risk of diluting the CBT. If the main focus is systemic work, important facets of CBT such as goal setting, reviewing homework and setting up behavioural experiments may be neglected. Similarly, including family members in CBT without working systemically or using the specific techniques of family therapy runs the risk of people feeling blamed, not addressing the beliefs and behaviours of family members which may be maintaining the problem or which may increase the likelihood of relapse, and neglecting effective, well-established therapeutic techniques. Further, simply asking family members to attend therapy sessions may not necessarily add to a reduction in the problem. MacFarlane (2001) notes that marital and family involvement in the treatment of OCD may be positive, but does not seem to reduce OCD symptomatology. The importance which is placed in individual CBT on working collaboratively and using Socratic techniques is at risk of being ignored if we regard parents and family members as potential co-therapists who need to be educated and then told how to carry out exposure tasks with young people, rather than exploring their beliefs and behaviours in more detail in an attempt to understand how the problem has developed.

CBT with families with OCD is currently an under-researched area. As discussed above, adding CBT interventions to family therapy sessions is unlikely to achieve optimal symptom reduction. Similarly, involving family members in CBT sessions in an ad hoc manner may not significantly reduce the OCD symptomatology either. This argues for the incorporation of current CBT skills beyond psychoeducation and exposure work when working with parents. Idiosyncratic, cognition-driven formulations of parental beliefs and behaviours with regard to the maintenance of the OCD should be developed and shared. These idiosyncratic formulations should then guide treatment and subsequent behavioural experiments, as well as the systems involved in the therapy sessions. The inclusion of family members in this way, using current cognitive therapy skills to make sense of why family members may be maintaining a problem, rather than prescribing exposure-based tasks, makes intuitive sense. Further research in this area is needed to determine whether this intuitively appealing strategy can be empirically validated. It may also be helpful to develop measures in addition to those measuring the young person's OCD symptomatology in order to determine the effect of these interventions, as family involvement in treatment may prove to have benefits that extend beyond the reduction of obsessional symptomatology.

- Cognitive behavioural and family systems therapy approaches to the treatment of OCD are not easily reconciled; a key advantage of the CBT approach is its specificity; family therapies also have well-developed techniques for including family members.
- Simply asking family members to attend therapy sessions may not necessarily add to a reduction in the problem.
- Idiosyncratic, cognition-driven formulations should be developed and shared; they should guide treatment, as well as which systems to work with.

The family life cycle and OCD

Many young people with OCD report that their symptoms either began or worsened at significant points in their lives, such as moving to secondary school or moving out of home for the first time. Stobie *et al.* (2007) examined the course of OCD in people who failed to respond to CBT for OCD and found that respondents reported an average age of OCD symptom onset of 16 years, which might have been associated with going to college or leaving school. This finding is compatible with the cognitive model of OCD (Salkovskis, 1985) which highlights the importance of responsibility in the development and maintenance of OCD. Young people may become vulnerable to developing OCD at life cycle points where they change their environments and experience a significant change in the level of responsibility which they are accorded. If the problem persists or worsens, that individual may fail to negotiate the life cycle targets appropriate to their developmental stage. In severe cases of OCD, individuals often appear to be stuck at the particular developmental stage where the OCD first began to significantly interfere with their lives. For example, if the OCD worsened in their teenage years, they might not achieve the developmental task of establishing autonomy traditionally associated with successfully negotiating this life cycle stage.

From a family perspective, disruption to an individual within the family system is likely to have repercussions on other members of the system, so that the fulfilment of the age-appropriate life cycle goals of other individuals within the system may be delayed or even disrupted completely. An example of this might be where a young person with OCD is unable to attend school and one of their parents has to give up work to be at home with them.

- Young people may become vulnerable to developing OCD at life cycle points where they change their environments and experience a shift in responsibility.
- OCD may prevent an individual from achieving appropriate life cycle targets.
- Fulfilment of the age-appropriate life cycle goals of other family members may also be delayed.

Who is the client?

The above highlights another issue for the therapist to consider prior to the sessions starting – namely, who is their client and what are the factors which have motivated different family members to attend? This may also be reviewed over the course of the sessions, but being explicit about this and establishing the expectations of the different family members from the outset is likely to reduce confusion and increase collaboration. Family members may attend for the following reasons:

- to complain about the young person, or separate from them, or blame them for the development of the problem or other problems in the family
- one family member may wish to be confirmed as having a better approach to tackling the obsessional problem than other members
- to learn more about obsessional problems and how to help the young person to deal with them
- to check whether they are doing the right thing
- to seek emotional support or assistance, or a combination of these points.

In some cases family members may be in broad agreement about wanting to tackle the obsessional problem. In others, certain family members (sometimes the young person) may not believe that the obsessional problem exists, or is the main problem which needs to be addressed within the family. The greater the level of agreement between family members, the easier the therapist's task becomes. It is very easy to become distracted from focusing on overcoming obsessional problems even when working with individuals. When working with families, therapists can easily become distracted by other issues. One way of staying on track is to set clear goals at the start of therapy and to review these regularly over the course of the sessions.

Establishing the expectations of family members from the outset is likely to reduce confusion and increase collaboration.

Goal setting

A potential starting point in drawing up goals with the family is discussion about the effect of the OCD on the family as a whole and on individual family members separately. Who has had to sacrifice what in response to the OCD, and what do they wish to do about this? What are the goals of the various family members – how do they differ and how do they link to the life cycle stages of these family members? As usual, it is helpful to construct SMART goals (Specific, Measurable, Attainable, Realistic, Timely) and to break these into short, medium and long-term goals. The therapist should also ask which family members will be responsible for ensuring which of the goals are carried out.

In instances where a family member has had OCD for many years, family members may be pessimistic about what can be achieved. These beliefs can have a very negative effect on the progress of the therapy sessions. Therapists need to respect what the family has to say about the problem and what needs to be done to overcome it, but also not buy into unhelpful beliefs and collaborate in the setting of goals which will not be sufficient to make lasting improvements. Where the goals of family members conflict substantially, this suggests the need for further discussion and later review of the goals, possibly after formulating. Should substantial differences remain, the therapist may need to consider who they are representing and who it will be helpful to include in the sessions. Where goals significantly differ between family members, the therapist should use a combination of education, formulation and discussion techniques in order to address the most significant points of difference. If this has been done and the family members continue to have wildly divergent goals, the therapist will need to continue based on an understanding of who their client is. It may be necessary not to continue with all of the family members if no agreement can be reached.

- The therapist should begin by discussing the effect of the OCD on the family as a whole and on individual members separately.
- Goals should be SMART and broken down into short, medium and long-term.
- If family members continue to have wildly divergent goals, it may be necessary to stop working with some family members.

Education

A significant difference between this form of CBT and some of the other manualised treatment approaches (e.g. March and Mulle, 1998) with regard to education is that the present approach does not stress biological factors in educating family members about OCD. The advantage of stressing biological and genetic components to OCD may be that it can lead clients to feel less to blame for their symptoms, which is obviously potentially very helpful. However, stressing biological mechanisms as underpinning OCD can be disempowering and promote pessimism about the ability to change the problem fundamentally. It can result in OCD being viewed as a long-standing problem which can be managed but never fully treated. Further, it may lead them to regard themselves as having something fundamentally wrong with them. This would conflict with the core thread of normalising and making sense of the problem which runs through the cognitive conceptualisation of OCD.

> The present approach does not stress biological factors in educating family members about OCD, as this may make young people pessimistic about their ability to change the problem. This could also conflict with the core thread of normalising which runs through the cognitive conceptualisation of OCD.

Applying a modified version of the Salkovskis model to working with families

Having dispensed useful information to the family regarding OCD and how it works, the therapist may then proceed to ask for a recent example of the problem, in order to formulate how it works and how the different family members respond to the problem. When working with a young person presenting with OCD, where a therapist suspects that family members may be involved in the maintenance of the problem, it may be helpful to construct several different formulations for different family members, and to consider how these feed into the OCD. A slightly modified version of the Salkovskis (1985) model might be useful for therapists to bear in mind as a formulatory template to guide questions (see Figure 7.1).

The therapist should first formulate a recent typical example provided by the young person. Once a clear understanding of the problem has been obtained, the discussion can then move on to explore a different family member's response to the obsessional problem. In this case, instead of an intrusive thought, image, urge or doubt, the trigger is likely to be the young person's compulsions or urge to engage in compulsions. The threat appraisal remains central to the formulation, but may be entirely different to the

124 *Stobie*

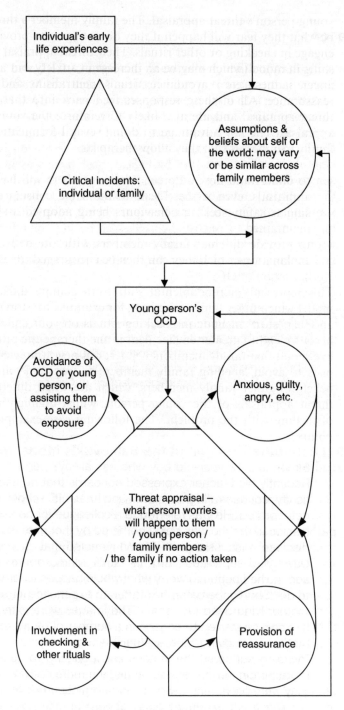

Figure 7.1 A modification of the Salkovskis model of OCD for use with family members

young person's threat appraisal. The family member's threat appraisal may be what they fear will happen if they do not agree to provide reassurance or engage in checking or other rituals. Their threat appraisal is likely to lead to shifts in mood (which may be an increase in anxiety, but also possibly guilt, anger, sadness, etc.), avoidance, rituals, neutralising and the provision of reassurance. All of these responses feed back into that family member's threat appraisal and are also likely to reinforce the young person's threat appraisal. The key advantage to doing several formulations with different family members is that they allow therapists:

- to understand how different family members will have different threat appraisals, even if these lead to the same consequences in terms of similar safety-seeking behaviours being adopted and the OCD being maintained
- to provide different family members with alternative, less threatening explanations which they can then be encouraged to test out.

This represents a fundamental shift from a more didactic, instructional model which urges family members, for example, to 'stop providing reassurance' or 'stop engaging in checking rituals on your child's behalf'. This is likely to lead to greater engagement in the therapeutic process, and a better likelihood that family members will test out new strategies. It enables therapists to avoid labelling family members as 'resistant', and normalises the beliefs of other family members, which are often different from the key threat appraisals of the young person, whilst highlighting different ways of dealing with the problem. The following case example illustrates these points.

> Simon is a 12-year-old boy who has always performed well at school. Recently his teacher expressed concerns that he had been having difficulty concentrating in class, and that his school performance had deteriorated. He was referred to a colleague for an assessment after he disclosed that he was being bothered by thoughts that he didn't wish to disclose. Discussion with Simon revealed that shortly after his mother Dawn had separated from his father Marco approximately two years ago, he had begun to worry what would happen to him if his mother were to die. Shortly thereafter he started to experience intrusive images of his mother lying dead in a coffin. The images were extremely upsetting to him and he started to engage in a number of rituals to try to prevent his mother from dying. These rituals included saying prayers in his head, trying to suppress the images and counting to 'lucky' numbers. The more Simon performed the rituals, the more convinced he became that they were preventing serious harm from occurring to his mother.
>
> Dawn felt extremely guilty about the difficulties which Simon was experiencing, partly as the worries centred on her, but also because she attributed Simon's difficulties to her separation from Marco. She had also had OCD as a child. In order to assuage her guilt, and to help

Simon, once she became aware of the problem she started to provide him with reassurance whenever he had the images. Unfortunately this developed into a pattern whereby Simon began to repeatedly ask her the same questions each night e.g. 'You're okay, aren't you Mum?'

Marco, who lived separately in the same town and had a new partner, looked after Simon on alternating weekends. Simon's therapist requested that he attend some of the initial sessions, as Dawn described his approach as being inconsistent with her approach to the problem. Marco reluctantly agreed to attend after being contacted by the therapist.

- A modified version of the Salkovskis (1985) model may be used as a formulatory template to guide questions.
- Different family members will have different threat appraisals, even if these lead to the same consequences in terms of similar safety-seeking behaviours.
- This model represents a shift from a didactic, instructional model to a more inquiring, collaborative way of working.

Formulating when working with an individual

The therapist began by formulating a recent typical example with Simon. Simon explained how he was staying at his father's home on Saturday evening when he suddenly had an image of the lid of a coffin being closed over his mother's face (intrusive image). The meaning of this image for Simon was the belief that this image could cause his mother to die (threat appraisal). This in turn led to him becoming extremely anxious (emotional response). He tried to count to his lucky number seven in his head and keep the seven stuck in his head (neutralising); he prayed that his mother would be all right (neutralising), tried to push the image out of his head (thought suppression) and phoned her to check that she was okay (checking ritual). All of these responses, including the anxiety, served to reinforce his belief that having these images meant that he could be responsible for causing serious harm to his mother, thereby reinforcing the threat appraisal and maintaining the OCD.

At some point in this process, the therapist may choose to complete another formulation – this time, based on the beliefs of a family member, rather than the young person. The therapist may choose to do this informally, using cognitive therapy discussion techniques to identify and challenge unhelpful beliefs and offer alternative, more helpful ways of seeing the problem. Alternatively, where an initial formulation has been done with the young person and found to be helpful, the therapist may choose to formally write up one or several more formulations that described the beliefs of different family members, and the way in which these beliefs affect their involvement in the problem. In this case, the trigger which activates the family member's threat appraisal is likely to be the young person's compulsive behaviour, rather than an intrusive thought. The family member's threat appraisal may be similar to, or differ significantly from, the young person's threat appraisal. Nonetheless, although the threat appraisals may differ, the emotional, physical and cognitive responses to the appraisals may be very similar to those of the young person and may also serve to reinforce or maintain the problem.

> - The therapist may choose to complete another formulation – this time based on the beliefs of a family member, rather than the young person.
> - The trigger activating the threat appraisal is likely to be the OCD, although the family member's threat appraisal may differ significantly from that of the young person.
> - However, the emotional, physical and cognitive responses to the appraisals may be very similar to those of the young person and may also maintain the problem.

Formulating from the perspective of family members

Having done some work with Simon in terms of formulating the problem and setting homework tasks, the therapist decided to see his parents individually to clarify their beliefs. It became apparent that Dawn felt guilty about the separation from Marco and partially believed that she had let Simon down by insisting on the separation. Within the formulation, the therapist identified the separation from Marco as a critical event which reinforced some longstanding beliefs which Dawn had about herself. Her son's compulsive behaviour was the trigger which then fed into two main threat appraisals: that Simon's OCD was her fault and that her son would no longer be able to function if he became too anxious. These appraisals led her to feel guilty and anxious. They also led her to provide her son with reassurance whenever possible, and to do everything in her power to try to help him to reduce all of his anxiety levels, including encouraging him to stay at home. Careful use of normalising and empathy was used by the therapist to illustrate how these responses were completely understandable, particularly within the context of her life history and the separation from Marco. However, the responses were only helpful if the beliefs were true. If they were untrue, and Dawn was a good mother to her son, who was not at risk of ceasing to function even if he became more anxious as a consequence of going out, then a different set of strategies was needed. The present ones were reinforcing these worrying beliefs, and possibly even contributing to Simon's obsessional problem, even though this was the last thing that Dawn wanted (see Figure 7.2).

The therapist also spent some time working separately with Simon's father Marco, who seemed to be the family member who was most resistant to Simon attending the therapy sessions. Marco's comments to Simon when he had tried to discuss the problem with his father were apparently dismissive. The therapist thought that using a formulatory approach might be helpful in gaining an understanding of why Marco, who was obviously very fond of his son, was seemingly not very supportive of him over the OCD.

Marco began the session by stating how angry he was with Dawn, as he was aware that that she had been spending a lot of time reassuring Simon, and he had read that reassurance only feeds the problem. He also believed that Dawn was using the obsessional problem to prevent Simon from seeing him on weekends, as Simon had become increasingly reluctant to stay over-night as he was worried about an accident befalling his mother whilst he was away. Marco was clearly very reluctant to believe that Simon had an obsessional problem. He stated that Simon's problems were 'a passing phase that all kids go through', citing how he used to play the game 'Step on a crack, break your mother's back' as a child. He believed the sessions were reinforcing the problem by 'making a big issue of it'. He also explained that his initial reluctance to attend the therapy sessions was due to the fear that he would be blamed for the problem.

Allowing Marco to express his concerns about Simon and the therapy sessions freed him up enough to allow the therapist to formulate a recent example illustrating his response to the obsessional problem. Marco cited an incident which had occurred the previous Saturday. He had hired *Shaun of the Dead* to watch with Simon. Unfortunately this spoof zombie movie had scared Simon and seemed to trigger his obsessional thoughts about harm coming to his mother. Simon began to experience intrusive images of his mother dying and turning into a zombie. He begged his father to take him home and started to engage in his neutralising rituals. Marco believed at this time that Simon was engaging in attention-seeking behaviour, which irritated him. He tried to rationalise with Simon and persuade him that nothing bad could possibly happen to his mother. When this failed to placate Simon, he encouraged him to try to suppress the thoughts and distract himself, which he had read was helpful (and the therapist explained was not). On seeing the level of distress that Simon was experiencing, Marco became increasingly upset and admitted that he feared his son was 'starting to lose it'. This was identified as Marco's main feared threat appraisal/belief, which caused him to feel anxious and guilty. Because this belief was so distressing and he did not know how to respond to it, he decided to take Simon back to Dawn. He also admitted to worrying constantly about his son, and that he had recently begun to avoid spending time with Simon as he found the obsessional problem very distressing to have to deal with.

The therapist discussed how Marco's responses to his beliefs about how Simon's behaviour was (a) attention-seeking and fostered by Dawn and (b) a

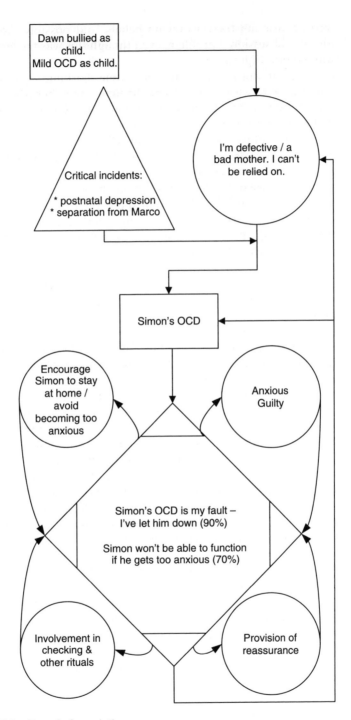

Figure 7.2 Dawn's formulation

sign of mental illness contradicted each other, and were also neither true nor helpful. She also helped him to see that although he had been trying hard to help Simon, his responses to these beliefs (encouraging suppression, distraction and rationalising, as well as becoming angry, returning Simon, and avoiding contact with him) were reinforcing his own beliefs and possibly also contributing to the obsessional problem, although this was the very last thing that he wanted.

The therapist used these formulations to wed her understanding of obsessional problems with the parents' beliefs about obsessional problems and their son, in order to make sense of the problem and their roles in it. The increased understanding which the formulations yielded the therapist and the family also led to a better rapport and greater consistency, and paved the foundations of further cognitive work, including theory A/B, revisiting goals and setting up specific behavioural experiments for family members based on their idiosyncratic concerns.

Theory A/B

The therapist worked with Simon, Marco and Dawn to contrast Simon's belief which was driving his compulsive behaviour with an alternative, less threatening explanation. The therapist argued that two possibilities existed and only one could be right – the problem was either *Theory A: having the images could cause his mother to die* (unless he neutralised them), or *Theory B: the problem was worry* (whatever thoughts or images he had couldn't cause his mother to die, whether he neutralised them or not). The therapist discussed, with family members present, how these two ways of looking at the problem are completely different. In the first, theory A, Simon was a potentially dangerous person with magical powers. In the second, theory B, he was a kind, caring son who worries too much about his thoughts and his parents. From here the therapist asked the family what evidence existed for both theories. She then challenged some of this evidence by encouraging Simon and his parents to have a discussion about what evidence would be admissible in a court of law (to separate spurious 'evidence' from real evidence). She then asked what action needed to be taken if each of the theories was true. If A were true, the family would need to help Simon to use all of their safety-seeking behaviours, avoidance, neutralising and reassurance-seeking rituals. If B were true, the family would need to encourage Simon to do the opposite, that is, to engage in day-to-day activities without avoidance, to take chances, to allow the thoughts to come and go freely, etc. (See Figure 7.3.)

The therapist worked separately with Dawn to establish her own theory A / theory B. In Dawn's case, theory A read 'The problem is I *am* a bad, uncaring mother who's caused Simon to have OCD' and theory B read 'The problem is I *worry* I'm a bad, uncaring mother who's caused Simon to have OCD – but actually I'm a really good mum who loves her son very much.'

Theory A The problem is having these pictures come into my head can cause Mum to die.	Theory B The problem is worry about these pictures.
Evidence for theory A • I feel really scared sometimes (actually, this fits better with theory B!). • Mum hurt her foot once after I'd had a bad picture (but maybe this wasn't because of me!).	*Evidence for theory B* • Although I've had lots of bad pictures and I haven't always been able to block them, nothing really bad has ever happened to Mum. • Other people get bad thoughts too sometimes. • I can't make good things happen by imagining them, so how can I make bad things happen? • Etc.
What do I need to do if A is true? • Try to block all my bad thoughts. • Say prayers. • Count to special numbers. • Think good thoughts all the time. • Always check that Mum is okay. • Don't go to school. • Etc.	*What do I need to do if B is true?* • Let myself think whatever I want to – even bad thoughts or pictures! • Go out lots. • Worry less about Mum. • Go to school. • Visit my friends and have fun. • Stay with Dad more. • Have fun trying experiments. • Etc.

Figure 7.3   Simon's theory A and theory B

The second part of this sentence was deliberately added by the therapist to help Dawn separate these two ways of perceiving herself, as her low self-esteem made this difficult for her to do. Evidence was then gathered and critically assessed for both theories. Dawn was also asked what she needed to do if A were true and if B were true, for herself and for Simon. She concluded that if A were true, she would need to constantly apologise to Simon and give him reassurance. She should doubt herself and her abilities and ruminate about this extensively and she should spend all her time with Simon worrying about him. If B were true, she should stop spending her time feeling guilty and ruminating and she should make more time for herself. The time spent with Simon should be 'quality time', unhampered by worry and doubt, which she could model for him by encouraging him to go out more and visit friends. Dawn was asked to draw up a similar theory A/B for herself based on her other threat appraisal, using theory A 'The problem is Simon will no longer be able to function if he becomes too anxious' and theory B 'The problem is *worry* that Simon will not be able to function – but in fact we are both a lot tougher than we give each other credit for!'

The amount of time that Marco had set aside to attend the sessions did not allow the therapist to write up a detailed theory A/B with him. However, the main threat appraisal which had been uncovered during the session with him was discussed using theory A/B as a template – theory A 'The problem is my son is cracking up and I can't deal with this' and theory B 'The problem is my son worries excessively about his mother and I worry about my ability to cope with this – although I have a good relationship with my son and have the ability to help him through this.' Evidence for theory A and B was discussed. Interestingly, Marco decided as a consequence that he needed to gather more evidence here and the only way of doing this would be to spend more time with Simon. This also tied in with what he concluded he would need to do if theory B were true, as the therapist believed.

Contrasting alternative, less threatening ways of perceiving the obsessional problem with the family members' threat appraisals using theory A and B paved the way for setting up and carrying out behavioural experiments to test the two opposing theories. The results were then fed back into further experiments, and the findings were linked back into the theory A/B framework.

- Theory A/Theory B is a useful technique for contrasting threat appraisals with the alternative, less threatening explanations provided by the therapist.
- This technique can highlight two conflicting ways of dealing with the problem, in order to encourage family members to tackle the problem in a uniform way.
- This can form the basis of future behavioural experiments.

Behavioural experiments

Simon, Marco and Dawn were encouraged to devise behavioural experiments to test out their beliefs about the problem and how it works. Because Simon was at first reluctant to test out anything which could potentially cause harm to his mother, the therapist modelled experiments for him which were initially based on trying to cause good things to happen by thinking them or imagining them as images. She then wished bad things on herself and on her family members, before encouraging Simon to have thoughts and images about her. The results were recorded very assiduously by Simon in his therapy book.

Dawn was also encouraged to devise and test her own behavioural experiments, most of which were focused on testing out the effects of not offering Simon reassurance and encouraging him to go out more. Because of her low confidence and self-esteem she was also encouraged to keep a positive data log, which provided her with very useful evidence in support of her as a capable, caring mother. Dawn also commented that she found the idea of finding different ways of being supportive to Simon other than by providing reassurance to be extremely useful (see Figure 7.4).

Situation	Experiment	How do I ensure the experiment is fair?	Predictions	Outcome	What did I learn? How can I take this forward?
Simon going to visit friend.	Encourage him to sleep over at his friend's house.	Don't keep texting him to check he is okay. Try to not reassure him that I'll be okay.	He'll get really anxious (95%). He'll burst into tears (70%). I'll feel terrible (100%). I'll have to go round and bring him home (90%).	Apparently he did become quite anxious at one point but then he soon settled. He didn't cry. I did worry about him a lot but I managed to not call or text him, and I didn't have to fetch him.	Simon's stronger than I give him credit for – although I'm not so sure about myself! Next time I'll worry about him less. I'll also visit a friend so that I spend less time worrying.

Figure 7.4 Dawn's behavioural experiment

Marco was similarly encouraged to set up and test out his own behavioural experiments, although he was initially reluctant to write these down. Nonetheless, he did devise some good experiments aimed at testing out his beliefs about his inability to help Simon with the obsessional problem. This empowered him and increased his confidence significantly. Carrying out the experiments also had a helpful side-effect, in that father and son spent more time together as a result. Having all of the family members involved in setting up and testing their own behavioural experiments also strengthened the externalisation of the obsessional problem, which enabled them to get on better with each other whilst fighting a common enemy with a united front.

- Family members can be encouraged to construct and carry out their own behavioural experiments.
- This engages family members in treatment, externalises the obsessional problem and can unite family members.

Discussion techniques

The results of the behavioural experiments were linked with cognitive discussion techniques such as questioning the mechanism of problems, identifying and challenging unhelpful assumptions and cognitive biases, discussing pros and cons, developing responsibility pie charts and other techniques discussed elsewhere in this book. In addition to these standard cognitive therapy techniques, the rich family therapy literature on questions can also be extremely helpful for therapists working with families with OCD. Different types of questions (e.g. circular or reflexive – see Tomm, 1988) can be used to highlight differences and similarities in the beliefs of family members, as well as the interaction between the behaviours and beliefs of family members on each other.

An illustration of this occurred when working with a family whose daughter had been worrying obsessionally that she would throw bleach into the milk of a nearby dairy. Midway through the therapy sessions the family was invited in for a review – at which point the father surprised the therapist by stating that because his daughter was making so much progress, he had started to consider removing the lock he had placed on her bedroom door to lock her in at night. Further questioning revealed that the father did not believe that his daughter would poison the milk at night if she was not locked into her bedroom (he was surprised to even be asked this). However, he did worry that she would not be able to sleep all night without the reassurance of being locked in. Circular questioning was used to draw explicit links between his belief, the locking of the door and the reinforcement of his daughter's view of herself as a dangerous individual who needs to be locked up.

> Family therapy questions can be extremely helpful for therapists working with families with OCD, to highlight differences and similarities in the beliefs of family members, as well as the interaction between the behaviours and beliefs of family members on each other.

Problems encountered when working with families

The above approach is intended to illustrate how the CBT techniques discussed elsewhere in this book can be easily adapted to working with families. It is worth noting that this approach will not always be applicable. It is most likely to be helpful when working with family members who have become involved in the maintenance of the problem, either due to a lack of understanding about how obsessional problems work, or due to their own concerns. However, it will often be the case that family members may be very supportive without being involved in the maintenance of the problem through the provision of reassurance, etc. Where this is the case, the therapist may wish to work individually with the young person, or involve family members as co-therapists. Therapists should also seek to reinforce effective familial support structures. Working with families also carries particular ethical responsibilities. Encouraging family members to disclose the content of their intrusive fears to each other can be crucial in overcoming the secrecy which often perpetuates OCD. However, working closely with family members can potentially place the therapist at risk of ethical transgressions, for example, when working with teenagers who do not wish the content of their obsessions to be disclosed to their parents.

Some family members may be actively critical of the young person and their compulsive rituals. If this hostility is active and rigid, they or the therapist may decide that their involvement in the therapy sessions would be counterproductive. Family members can sometimes be supportive of each other but have significantly different goals. Some family members who elect not to involve themselves in compulsive rituals as a consequence of the sessions may alienate themselves from others, exacerbating rifts in the family. Family members whose relationships with the young person were previously defined by their involvement in the rituals may sometimes find it difficult to adjust once the OCD improves.

Lastly, the therapist may struggle when encountering cross-generational shared familial values (whether cultural, religious or more general). Therapists may struggle to persuade family members to test out behavioural experiments which require them to challenge some of these beliefs. In this instance it is often helpful to enlist members of the wider system, e.g. grandparents, friends (through surveys) or members of the wider community, to find out whether the familial beliefs and customs are shared by other representative members of the broader group to which the family belongs.

- This approach is likely to be helpful when working with family members who have become involved in the maintenance of the problem.
- Where family members are supportive but not involved in rituals or the provision of support, individual therapy sessions may be preferable.

8

Issues and future directions in childhood OCD

Paul M. Salkovskis, Polly Waite and Tim Williams

For the young people we work with, their future lies in getting rid of their OCD.

'It's weird not having OCD. It's a lot more free and I don't feel so weighed down. I can focus a lot more on things because I'd pushed things like schoolwork to the side, but that would add to the weight of it because it would still be there in the back of my mind annoying me. I have a lot more thinking time and I think "What shall I think about now because I've got nothing to worry me?" It's quite good. I'm busier, full of energy and have other things to do to take up the space filled by compulsions and stuff. I can take new opportunities and I'm doing things now that I couldn't have done with OCD. I can go to bed quickly and go to sleep and if I don't feel like brushing my teeth I won't. General things like that, I can choose what I want to do.'

'OCD is not easy to overcome. It takes time, patience and understanding but it is worth it. It was like a weight being lifted. OCD is frustrating and CBT can be emotional but it does help and work. Since getting rid of the OCD, my self-confidence has improved vastly and since I started sixth form people say to me how much they have noticed it too. Also I now socialise with friends and participate in school social events. My family also comment on how happy I am.'

'At the beginning of therapy I was scared and worried and also upset to discuss my OCD. As time went on I learnt that I could beat and control the OCD. I did activities like putting my hand down a loo and then licking it to prove I wouldn't get ill or die from germs as I believed. Therapy was worth it because I found myself as a person in control and independent with life. Also it helped me recognise that just because I had OCD I am no different from any other person without it. I now think more positive.

I now have determination to do what I want and also achieve what I want.'

These are the same three young people who described their OCD in Chapter 1, but this time describing how it feels to be rid of OCD. Taken together with the growing body of treatment outcome research, they establish the all important point: OCD can be cured – not just improved, not 'learning to live with the problem', but cured. The facts that it can at times be difficult, time consuming, incomplete, expensive and harrowing for all concerned do not detract from the simple observation that it can be done. This being so, the future needs to hold a new set of apparently achievable aspirations: how to cure childhood OCD earlier, more efficiently, in more people and more easily. It is also important to recognise that we need to work out how to help those young people who 'partially respond'. To achieve these goals, we need to achieve a better understanding not only of factors involved in the origins and maintenance of OCD and the way in which it manifests, but also those which relate to the process of achieving and sustaining excellent treatment response.

A theme running through the work described in this book is the importance of reducing the young person's worries, not only by helping them to discover that the things they fear will not happen, but also, at the same time, by providing them with an alternative, less threatening explanation of their difficulties. The girl who was afraid of contamination comes to see that it is the fear and not the contamination which is her problem, and goes on to overcome that fear by confronting rather than escaping contamination. The boy who feared that harm would come to his mother because of the thoughts he had is helped to see that he is not causing harm but fears it, and that fear can be dealt with without seeking to neutralise frightening thoughts. CBT emphasises the way in which 'loosening up' beliefs makes it easier to change behaviour, and that changes in behaviour further loosen up the beliefs. It is also clear that one of the belief changes that is crucial relates to 'normalisation'; helping the young person see how their ideas about the problem showing that they are weird, mad or bad are incorrect and indeed almost the opposite – that they are caring and sensitive individuals with much to offer. Another key component of effective treatment is an implication of the previous points; that it is important for the young person not only to disengage from their worries, but to engage more fully in positive aspects of their life, including renewing their ambitions, hopes and dreams.

It is now clear that the majority of young people who receive an adequate dose of well-conducted CBT do well, and do not need much further help to keep OCD at bay. However, the challenges that face us include the need to further develop our understanding and ability to change several key areas:

1   We have only an incomplete understanding of how developmental issues link to the development and treatment of OCD in young people.
2   Sufferers, their families and teachers often fail to recognise the onset of OCD.

3   OCD can provoke negative reactions in the sufferer and those around
     them when recognised.
4   OCD is too often seen as untreatable.
5   Treatment is scarce and difficult to access, usually with very long delays.
6   The quality of CBT offered is often extremely poor.

Developmental issues

Not surprisingly, treatments for OCD in young people are a spin-off from
work with adults and inevitably modifications are required, with the risk that
some elements of treatment become 'lost in translation'. By the same token,
it seems likely that some entirely new elements may be required for young
people in order to achieve the same goals as in adults. It almost goes without
saying that development and adaptation of treatment depends on an understanding of the cognitive abilities and capacities of young people. This is not
only a problem to be solved, but also an advantage to be exploited. The fact
that young people are in a state of flux in terms of their beliefs and particularly open to new learning (relative to the more rigid cognitive structures of
adults) is a positive factor which could be better utilised.

In terms of assessment, one of the main challenges is to determine
whether obsessional thinking and compulsive behaviours reflect a variant of
normal development, OCD or some other clinical problem. A thorough
detailed assessment with high levels of validity is key in determining this.
Children as young as three years may be referred with repetitive behaviours
and while some of these, such as head-banging or rocking themselves to
sleep at night have little to do with OCD, others such as touching objects or
rituals may be intended to prevent harm occurring and reflect OCD. It is all
the more difficult when young people may struggle to articulate their beliefs
or explain why they are carrying out certain behaviours. Clinicians need to
develop ways of gathering information (including, but not confined to, asking understandable questions) in order to understand what the young person
is experiencing and what treatment strategies may be most appropriate. It
seems clear that the kind of beliefs which appear to motivate obsessional
behaviour in adults are present in children, but that younger children find it
harder to articulate them.

In general, the literature on OCD in young people does not systematic-
ally distinguish between early, pre-pubertal onset and adolescent onset and
so it still remains unclear as to whether the course and outcome of OCD in
these two groups is the same. Studies on early onset OCD in people assessed
in adulthood suggest that early onset is more likely to be co-morbid with tic
disorders (e.g. Geller *et al.*, 1998) and it may be that this is quite different to
the OCD developed later on. However, most studies in this field are difficult
to interpret because of sampling problems. In our clinical experience, the
compulsions seen in some of our younger people may be carried out for
reasons rather less obviously focused on reducing objectively serious harm
(e.g. death of self or a parent), and more focused on gaining control over
their environment. In the latter instance, the course of treatment has been

rather different to other young people with OCD and some of these young-sters have gone on to develop externalising disorders, such as oppositional defiant disorder. If there are different subtypes of OCD, it is crucial that we understand them better, which in turn should have important implications for treatment. As with other types of anxiety-related avoidance, ritualising and compulsive behaviours can represent a 'final common pathway'. For example, panic patients and patients with severe osteoporosis both tend to show agoraphobic avoidance as a result of their fear of the consequences of being out of the house; the basis of the feared catastrophe motivating avoid-ance is however quite different.

- We have only an incomplete understanding of how devel-opmental issues link to the development and treatment of OCD in young people.
- Treatments are a 'spin-off' from work with adults and inevitably modifications are required.
- It is likely that some entirely new elements will be needed with younger people to achieve the same goals as in adults.

Understanding thinking patterns across age ranges

We have some understanding of maintenance but little information about the origins of OCD

A number of studies (e.g. Barrett and Healy, 2003; Libby *et al.*, 2004) suggest that the beliefs which characterise OCD in adults, such as inflated responsi-bility and the closely linked concept of overimportance of thoughts, are also present in young people. However, reliance on studies that pool data from young people across broad age ranges means that we are unclear as to how beliefs manifest at particular ages and how they evolve. We have much to learn about how both intrusive thoughts and their appraisals develop and everything to learn about how they begin.

It is widely recognised that most people (including young children) experience personally unacceptable intrusive thoughts, images, impulses and doubts, and it is self-evidently true that OCD develops when the young person fails to learn to disregard such intrusions. However, what is less clear is why some young people are able to disregard them and others are not. A leading view is that it relates to the young person becoming aware of their own 'agency'; that is, once they become aware they can cause bad things to happen, it is a corollary that they have the ability to make bad things not happen by what they do. However, it is also clear that superstitious ideas (such as bad things happening if cracks in the pavement are stepped on) are common enough to be regarded as part of normal development. It may be that more fundamental beliefs and values are involved in the appraisals linked to the development of OCD. Identifying these is difficult in adults and likely to be more difficult still in younger age groups. Such issues are likely to be important if early intervention and prevention are to be considered.

It has been suggested that cognitive factors may be less important in younger children and that compulsions may be more habitual and driven by a physical urge. In such instances, it is suggested that a cognitive explanation may develop in an attempt to give meaning to the behaviour rather than as a motivator. We believe this conclusion is based on inappropriate assessment of cognition in young children. There is a clear need to develop more sophisticated assessment strategies appropriate to such children's abilities to communicate the beliefs they have.

Vulnerability and aetiological factors in obsessional problems

As with other psychiatric problems, we have a great deal of data concerning factors associated with OCD, with these probably being involved in the maintenance of the problem. In some instances (such as responsibility appraisals) it can also reasonably be hypothesised that these factors may be part of the origins of OCD, but it is much harder to establish causal links as opposed to associations. There is little in the way of purely empirical or descriptive data on the aetiology of OCD, so much of our limited theoretical understanding has to come from generalisations of the theory.

The cognitive theory of the development of obsessional disorder suggests that, as a result of prior experience, the individual develops particular assumptions (particularly about their own thinking and what this means, but also about issues surrounding prevention of harm and responsibility for it). These assumptions may be self-evidently problematic (sometimes) or may initially appear to be innocuous (more commonly). At some later time, the occurrence of a particular critical incident or series of such incidents has the effect of activating the assumptions, leading to appraisals linked to responsibility for harm by what is done or not done. Such critical incidents are defined as events or situations which activate the previously 'silent' assumptions. Usually this means that critical incidents 'mesh' with beliefs; e.g. the incident or situation fulfils the conditions inherent in the assumption. The development of attempts to resist, to avoid and to neutralise (also regarded as linked to such assumptions) triggers maintenance cycles as defined in the theory.

Salkovskis *et al.* (1999) have proposed that several patterns of belief and experience may be involved in the origins of OCD (or vulnerability to its development), but highlighted the problems in researching such issues in the clinic, where people typically present between 7 and 12 years after the onset of their problems, rendering attempts to identify the origins particularly problematic. However, working with a younger age group may offer new opportunities for investigation of the origins of OCD. By definition, young people living under the care of their parents are likely to come to professional attention much earlier than independent adults, as parents spot changes in their behaviour, mood or attitudes and seek help on the young person's behalf.

In most instances, the evolution of obsessional symptoms and linked beliefs is likely to be a subtle and interactive process taking place over many years in ways which are hard to detect even for the young person themselves. We have previously identified a set of more obvious patterns that are likely to be relatively easy to detect on the basis of retrospective or concurrent self-report. Five patterns are suggested: note that some, but not all, are mutually exclusive:

1   An early developed and broad sense of perceived responsibility for avoiding threat which has been deliberately or implicitly encouraged and promoted during childhood by parental significant figures and circumstances, leading to enduring and 'justified' beliefs about the importance of a sense of responsibility.
2   Rigid and extreme codes of conduct and duty, including religious and moral principles.
3   Childhood experience in which sensitivity to ideas of responsibility develops as a result of being shielded from it. This may include over-indulgence (being spoiled) and/or may be the consequence of the implication or by the communication by those around them that the child is in some sense incompetent.
4   A specific incident or series of incidents in which actions or inaction actually contributed in a significant way to a serious misfortune that affects oneself or, often more importantly, others (e.g. being involved in a causal chain resulting in injury or death, such as distracting someone who then has an accident or placing an object somewhere that later harms someone).
5   An incident in which it wrongly appeared that one's thoughts and/or actions or inaction contributed to a serious misfortune (e.g. wishing that someone comes to harm, then this 'coming true').

Other factors may also contribute, including actual or perceived criticism, acute or sudden increases in levels of personal responsibility and additional experiences of the type described in points (3) and (4) above:

1   *Criticism and blame.* An experience of systematic criticism and/or scape-goating may contribute to the development of an inflated sense of responsibility. The criticism may be parental in origin, or may occur at school. We suggest that criticism will increase the subjective cost of being responsible, for example, 'If I make a mistake, people will blame me.' That is, there is an additional consequence to not acting in a responsible manner. Note that this does not imply that criticism alone is sufficient to create an inflated sense of responsibility.
2   *Increased levels of responsibility.* In people who are already predisposed to such beliefs, a situational increase in responsibility may lead to an inflated sense of responsibility. There are at least two patterns. In the

first, the number of responsible roles gradually creeps up incrementally where the person acquires additional obligations or duties. These obligations or duties may be imposed, but among those who already have a strongly developed sense of responsibility, they may be willingly accepted or actively sought out. In the second, the level of responsibility may jump rapidly with a change in circumstances such as the transition from a two parent to single parent family, moving from primary to secondary school, and so on.

3   *Activating or coincidental events.* Incidents involving real or perceived responsibility or blame for events causing harm, perceived 'near misses', or coincidental events that are interpreted as the person having caused harm can all create an inflated sense of personal responsibility by themselves. However, in combination with the patterns of development discussed above, such events or additional events of these types may further inflate responsibility. Such events have previously been characterised as 'critical incidents'. Such incidents would not in themselves necessarily trigger obsessional problems. However, these events (they are often, but not only, adverse life events) can combine and 'mesh' with pre-existing attitudes and assumptions to trigger responsibility appraisals and the factors which may serve to maintain such appraisals.

Clearly, understanding causal factors better is likely to facilitate both primary and secondary prevention. However, before such ambitious undertakings are implemented, the empirical basis of causal factors needs to be established. Data on parenting styles in OCD has produced little evidence of a particular pattern of parental behaviour or interaction. However, based on the current analysis, more than one parenting style could contribute to an inflated sense of responsibility. An implication of the present analysis is that, if both being given too much responsibility and too little responsibility can contribute, then measures taken from these hypothesised subgroups could well cancel each other out in an overall analysis. It may be more useful to use cluster analysis or other such as semi-ideographic strategies to establish meaningful profiles leading to OCD as a 'final common pathway'. Development of an inflated sense of responsibility may for some people be best modelled as accumulating experiences that individually may have relatively little effect.

- We have some understanding of maintenance but little information about the origins of OCD and so much of our limited theoretical understanding has to come from generalisations of the theory.
- We need to establish an empirical basis of causal factors in order to facilitate treatment and prevention.

Understanding co-morbidity

From clinical experience we know that individuals rarely present to services with one clear-cut psychological problem. This is supported by research which indicates that young people with OCD often have other psychological problems. Studies suggest that three-quarters of young people also meet criteria for other diagnoses (March *et al.*, 2004; Swedo and Rapoport, 1989), with anxiety disorders and depression especially common. Despite this, our understanding of co-morbidity is poor. There appears to be considerable overlap in the thinking patterns in OCD and other phenomena such as worry and yet it is unclear as to whether these really are different, distinct pathologies or, as seems likely, whether by using a diagnostic system we are making artificial divisions.

In terms of treatment (and to some extent theory), co-morbidity is probably best dealt with by formulation. The patterns involved vary. We have been able to identify situations where a single factor causes multiple problems (e.g. clinical perfectionism as a vulnerability factor for OCD, eating disorders and depression; cf Shafran *et al.*, 2003). Most commonly, one problem triggers another (e.g. as OCD makes more and more inroads into the young person's life and prevents them from engaging in normal activities, they become more and more demoralised until they meet clinical criteria for depression). Rarer, but importantly, another problem is primary and OCD is secondary; for example, depression and grief trigger obsessional symptoms. In such instances, establishing the timeline is crucial in order to decide which problems should be treated first. In some instances, co-morbidity simply represents the person having two separate problems, in the way that it is possible to have both influenza and chickenpox at the same time. The complication in such instances can be that although initially functionally independent, the problems may begin to interact as time goes by.

> Young people with OCD often have other psychological problems and this co-morbidity is probably best dealt with by individual case formulation.

Establishing the role of biological factors

The literature on obsessional problems in general and childhood OCD in particular emphasises the idea that OCD is a 'neurodevelopmental disorder'. 'Theoretical' papers emphasising biological explanations abound. Curiously, this enthusiasm for biological approaches has not resulted in coherent biological theories and the evidence for biological discontinuity for OCD is largely absent.

A common clinical justification for the use of biological explanations is that in some way it is 'good for the patient'. Those advocating this position argue that biological disease models are destigmatising and empowering relative to psychological models. Promoting the view that mental health problems have biological causes has become an established part of many programmes with the declared intention of reducing stigma. However, the promotion of biological factors is not necessarily in the best interest of those with mental health problems and their families. For example, genetic factors may be promoted (or overpromoted) as causal with little regard for the potential impact that such ideas may have (Rimes and Salkovskis, 1998). Clinicians, sufferers and carers who uncritically consider genetic factors are likely to overestimate these. Once a person is identified as having OCD, relatives will recall great uncle George who was funny about being clean. Cousin Emily was diagnosed as having OCD. The young person's grandmother recalls an aunt who checked a lot. Three cases in a family, that sounds like a lot. However, the context is that the collective recollection of family members of several generations can draw upon a potential pool of information about almost 200 relatives; OCD is likely to occur at normal lifetime rates in at least eight of those. If obsessional symptoms are included the figure would rise to somewhere in the region of 30. None of the examples given are first-degree relatives. Note also that genetic and biological explanations may have the effect of alleviating feelings of blame and guilt not in the young person but in the parents.

Biological accounts can be problematic because they may have the unwanted effect of inducing pessimism regarding likely treatment outcome in young people, their carers and the general public. Attributing mental health problems to 'brain disease' and biological causes additionally affects the extent to which sufferers are regarded as unusually unpredictable, potentially antisocial or even frankly dangerous by and to themselves and others. The brain is commonly understood to be the organ of the mind and the 'seat of the self'; a diseased brain for many comes to mean a diseased mind and diseased 'self'.

Research in an adult community sample highlighted that 'psychological' but not 'biological' labels resulted in more positive views of mental health problems relative to controls (Lam *et al.*, 2005). Anxious and depressed patients have also been shown to be similarly susceptible to biological labelling effects in experimental studies (e.g. Lam and Salkovskis, 2007). The importance of clinicians' attitudes to causal factors in mental health problems lies both in their own expectations of patients' response to treatment (Lam *et al.*, submitted) and in the extent to which their causal beliefs are transmitted to patients. The way in which patients understand and accept such causal explanations may in turn affect not only their expectation of change, but also their engagement and response in treatment. Understanding how causal labelling might affect younger people with mental health problems is thus an important next step in research terms. To our knowledge, there are no data on children's reaction to causal labelling. OCD has been an area in which such labelling has been particularly prominent since the publication of the popular book *The Boy Who Couldn't Stop Washing* (Rapoport, 1989).

In order to understand OCD in young people better, we may need to consider neuroscience-based approaches to establishing the role of biological/genetic factors and their interaction in the type of way that has been done in complex trait research (Kovas and Plomin, 2006). Disease/neuropsychiatric models (e.g. comparing OCD to neurological disease such as epilepsy or genetic problems such as Huntington's disease) have failed to help our understanding and may well have been damaging in terms of stigma. Currently, biological theories struggle to account for the specific phenomenology of OCD and the effectiveness of psychological treatment. This is not to say that biological factors are not relevant, as all psychological processes have a physiological substrate. The mistake, in our view, is to presume a pathophysiological basis of OCD.

To progress our understanding of OCD, biological accounts need to be conceived of in a more subtle way. The fact that psychological theories and research are so well developed should provide a useful starting point, allowing consideration of the psychological/neurophysiological interface. Such theories may be able to generate specific predictions based on the phenomenology of OCD and therefore provide evidence to evaluate them. It thus seems extremely unlikely at this stage that OCD will be identified as a primarily biological abnormality, making the interface between normal biological and psychological factors and how these normal processes can produce disordered reactions of the type seen in OCD the primary area of interest. Such research may suggest ways in which psychological and pharmacological treatments might be combined synergistically in particular types of problem. Note that at present CBT is the first line treatment, with the combination of psychological and pharmacological treatment being of uncertain value.

- Although 'theoretical' papers emphasising biological explanations abound, this has not resulted in coherent biological theories.
- Biological accounts can be problematic in that they may have the unwanted effect of inducing pessimism regarding likely treatment outcome and lead to stigma.
- The primary area of interest may be the interface between normal biological and psychological factors and how these processes can produce disordered reactions as seen in OCD.

Understanding family involvement

Unsurprisingly, research on treatment of young people with OCD suggests that family factors may be relevant in understanding the problem and seeking to change it. There is evidence that families of young people with OCD are more likely to be characterised by high levels of criticism and overinvolvement (Hibbs *et al.*, 1991) and lower levels of emotional support (Valleni-Basile *et al.*, 1995). Families of young people with OCD have demonstrated less use of positive problem solving and been less likely to reward independence in their children (Barrett *et al.*, 2002). There may also be other factors that are important, such as families holding strong and rigid belief systems (e.g. overvaluing cleanliness or setting overly high standards). However, it is unclear how these factors are involved in the development and maintenance of the problem. It is possible that these factors contribute towards the development of OCD, in that if young people are given less responsibility and support, they may be less able to use their own resources effectively to deal with difficulties. Alternatively, these factors may be involved more in the maintenance of the problem, as OCD disrupts family relationships and functioning and families often find themselves in a vicious cycle, where they accommodate the OCD and become involved in providing reassurance or carrying out compulsions. The stress of having a family member suffering from OCD may distort family relationships, rendering them more abnormal and stressful for the sufferer, which in turn may exacerbate the obsessional problem.

What is clear is that there is little evidence of direct transmission of OCD from parents to children. Surprisingly few children of parents suffering from OCD develop this problem either as a child or later. Direct copying of symptoms is unlikely to be an explanation of childhood OCD. Challacombe and Salkovskis (submitted) evaluated children of women with OCD, finding little evidence of elevated anxiety levels relative to healthy controls and an anxious comparison group. Observation of parent–child interaction revealed some differences in terms of the granting of autonomy which might be expected to predispose the child to the experience of anxiety symptoms later in their development. However, it seems likely that the level of risk to children of women suffering from OCD is rather low.

> Although family factors have been put forward as relevant in understanding OCD, it remains unclear how they are involved in both the development and maintenance of OCD.

Future opportunities

Prevention

As we develop a greater understanding of the nature and development of OCD, the clear implication is that this understanding may provide opportunities for prevention or the development of primary or secondary prevention strategies. Quite what form this should take is unclear, but at this stage leading candidates would be to teach young people about the nature of intrusive thoughts and to learn to ignore them rather than to think of them as meaningful and occurrences to be 'neutralised'. Learning about the uncontrollability of intrusive thoughts, images and doubts and the controllability of responses to them may be able to prepare young people to deal with intrusions more effectively. If we can understand the kind of things which mark the transition from normal intrusive thoughts to obsessional disorders, we may be able to help and support them to deal with these situations, thereby reducing the likelihood of OCD developing. The clearest examples of triggers in young people include bullying, peer relationship problems and illness or death within the family. Previously held or newly developed beliefs (such as overly rigid moral codes, ideas about thought–action fusion) are a further obvious target of preventative interventions.

More broadly, if we were to teach young people some of what they would learn in CBT (such as normalising of intrusions) and to use some of the techniques such as behavioural experiments to test out predictions about the way their thinking and behaviour impacts on the world, it may be possible to reduce the rate of people going on to develop different disorders. Historically, these questions are left unanswered as research of this kind is difficult to do. This is because the prevalence of OCD is around 1 per cent or less in teenagers and so in order to determine whether prevention programmes have any real effect, sample sizes would need to be extremely large or risk predictions particularly strong. Nevertheless, it makes good sense to work with young people to enable them to deal effectively with distressing thoughts, worries and their reactions to adverse life events through educational settings, youth groups and other environments, as well as through print and broadcast media.

> As we develop a greater understanding of the nature and development of OCD, this may provide opportunities for primary and secondary prevention strategies.

Developing and refining treatment

Despite the success of CBT, many young people with OCD fail to make progress in treatment or have difficulty maintaining progress over the longer term. In order to improve treatment, we need to understand better what might define the problems experienced by those young people who do poorly in therapy. Rachman (1983) describes how in some cases the individual does not improve because the treatment is inadequate or not adequately delivered, which he calls 'technical treatment failures'. This is a kind way of indicating that some therapists do not do treatment very well. In other cases, treatment may be delivered adequately but the individual makes limited progress and these are described as 'serious treatment failures'. Clearly identifying factors likely to result in relatively poorer outcomes will, in research terms, allow research to turn failure into success.

In clinical settings, there is often an assumption that many of the difficulties in treatment arise from secondary complications, such as poor motivation, and are down to the individual rather than the therapist. This can be seen as a type of self-serving cognitive bias on the part of the therapist. However, Stobie *et al.*'s (2007) study suggested that it was technical failures which were extremely common and advocated specialist training and supervision for clinicians in CBT, as well as the development and use of quality assurance measures to ensure that individuals are actually receiving what they are being offered. With young people in particular, it may be that some of these technical failures are related to difficulty with engagement and it is vital that clinicians are approachable, use the right language, listen respectfully and adapt therapy appropriately according to the age and development of the child.

Little is currently known about why some young people make little progress with adequate treatment, although co-morbidity and family factors may be involved. The idea that 'one size fits all' in terms of therapy is, of course, risible. Research in adult OCD indicates that co-morbidity (e.g. Axis II, 'personality disorders') does not usually prevent therapeutic change with treatment when the main problem is an anxiety disorder. However, such patients tend to have more severe problems and at the end of standardised treatment packages are more symptomatic than patients who do not show such co-morbidity. Further treatment sessions typically result in further change and the achievement of a similar end state.

There have been some attempts to provide family CBT, where as well as attending the therapy sessions, parents are also given skills training. However, there is not currently sufficient evidence that this is any more effective than individual CBT. Given that the family factors which appear to be relevant in understanding OCD in young people are poorly specified and understood, we remain unclear as to how family interventions might be deployed other than simply to deal with anxious parenting styles and encourage more adaptive behaviour in the affected young person. By the same token, if co-morbidity is of particular relevance, we need to consider whether by addressing these factors in treatment we can improve outcome. Future research needs to focus on the development of our theoretical understanding of these factors and then refining treatment to target particular issues.

- In order to improve treatment, we need to understand better what might define the problems experienced by those young people who do poorly in therapy.

- Future research needs to focus on the development of our theoretical understanding of factors that may be involved (such as co-morbidity or family factors) and then refining treatment to target particular issues.

The provision and dissemination of treatment

Studies on OCD in adults suggest that it is typically many years after obsessional symptoms significantly interfere before a diagnosis is made (e.g. Hollander, 1997; Stobie *et al.*, 2007). With young people, as in adults, presentation to clinical services tends to be rather late in the natural history of the problem if it happens at all. A range of factors can contribute to unwillingness to seek professional help, including fear of or shame about revealing what they are experiencing to others. Families can sometimes actively ignore symptoms, trying to reassure themselves and their child that there is nothing wrong and resisting seeking treatment because of the concerns of what a diagnosis may bring in terms of stigma and blame. For professionals to reach a greater proportion of young people who would benefit from treatment, we need to change the way mental health problems are perceived. As mentioned already, the most obvious way of achieving this is likely to be through a greater awareness of OCD and the effectiveness of treatment in both educational and primary care settings. Strategies designed to reduce the stigma of mental health problems in general and OCD in particular are needed; careful media work and work with the anxiety disorder charities are promising in this respect. For young people in particular, it is especially beneficial when 'celebrities' whom they admire and identify with talk openly about having OCD.

Currently, guidelines from the National Institute for Health and Clinical Excellence (NICE) for the treatment of OCD recommend a stepped care approach. This approach advocates beginning with the least expensive and intrusive interventions and moving on to more intensive treatment as and when necessary. In OCD, NICE suggests beginning with self-help for young people where the OCD is mild, but as yet there is no evidence base for this and self-help literature for young people with OCD is not generally available. There are risks associated with low-intensity treatments, in that a failure to respond could have a negative impact on the young person's self-esteem and reduce their motivation to continue to try to change, discouraging them from seeking subsequent treatment. It may also undermine their response to further treatment or lead to them being seen as 'untreatable' by professionals if they have already received some version of CBT.

NICE guidelines recommend CBT for young people with moderate to severe OCD or for those with mild OCD for whom self-help has been ineffective. These recommendations are based on the evidence from randomised controlled trials. However, it is unclear how generalisable these findings are, as the therapy carried out in research trials is unlikely to reflect general clinical practice. Typically studies involve highly skilled therapists in specialist settings and this is not normally available in routine clinical settings. It is now recognised that we need to expand access to CBT, but to do this it is vital that therapists are qualified and adequately trained to ensure that young people with OCD get the best possible treatment.

- We need to reach a greater proportion of young people who would benefit from treatment.
- In particular, strategies to reduce the stigma of mental health problems in general, and OCD in particular, are needed.
- We need to improve the availability of good quality CBT to ensure that young people with OCD get the best treatment possible.

In conclusion, the treatment of OCD in childhood has advanced greatly over the last decade from a state of stigmatising pessimism to heady optimism. There are many opportunities to extend our treatments to those who previously did not respond; for more effective and efficient treatment implementation; for disseminating effective treatments; and perhaps even early intervention and prevention. There seems now to be a real possibility that the work described in this book may have the effect of changing the epidemiology of OCD in children and young people. As if that were not good enough, it is also clear that doing so would reduce the prevalence of OCD throughout the age range. Now that would be a very fine thing to achieve.

References

Abela, J.R.Z., Brozina, K. and Haigh, E.P. (2002). An examination of the response styles of depression in third- and seventh-grade children: a short-term longitudinal study. *Journal of Abnormal Child Psychology, 30*, 515–527.

Abramowitz, J.S. (1996). Variants of exposure and response prevention in the treatment of obsessive-compulsive disorder: a meta-analysis. *Behaviour Therapy, 27*, 4, 583–600.

Abramowitz, J.S. and Foa, E.B. (2000). Does co-morbid major depression influence outcome of exposure and response prevention for OCD? *Behaviour Therapy, 31*, 795–800.

Allsopp, M. and Verduyn, C. (1988). A follow-up of adolescents with obsessive compulsive disorder. *British Journal of Psychiatry, 154*, 829–834.

Allsopp, M. and Williams, T. (1991). Self-report measures of obsessionality, depression and social anxiety in a school population of adolescents. *Journal of Adolescence, 14*, 149–157.

Allsopp, M. and Williams, T.I. (1996). Intrusive thoughts in a non-clinical adolescent population. *European Child and Adolescent Psychiatry, 5*, 1, 25–32.

American Psychiatric Association (APA, 1994). *Diagnostic and statistical manual of mental disorders* (4th edn), Washington, DC: American Psychiatric Association.

Arnold, L.M., McElroy, S.L., Mutasim, D.F., Dwight, M.M., Lamerson, C.L. and Morris, E.M. (1998). Characteristics of 34 adults with psychogenic excoriation. *Journal of Clinical Psychiatry, 59*, 10, 509–514.

Aronowitz, B.R., Hollander, E., DeCaria, C., Cohen, L., Saoud, J., Stein, D., *et al.* (1994). Neuropsychology of obsessive-compulsive disorder: preliminary findings. *Neuropsychiatry, Neuropsychology and Behavioural Neurology, 7*, 2, 81–86.

Asbahr, F.R., Castillo, A.R., Ito, L.M., Latorre, O., Moreira, M.N. and Lotufo-Neto, F. (2005). Group cognitive-behavioral therapy versus sertraline for the treatment of children and adolescents with obsessive-compulsive disorder. *Journal of the American Academy of Child and Adolescent Psychiatry, 44*, 1128–1136.

Barrett, P.M., Dadds, M.M. and Rapee, R.M. (1996a). Family treatment of childhood anxiety: a controlled trial. *Journal of Consulting and Clinical Psychology, 64*, 333–342.

Barrett, P.M. and Healy, L.J. (2003). An examination of the cognitive processes involved in childhood obsessive-compulsive disorder. *Behaviour Research and Therapy*, *41*, 286–299.

Barrett, P.M., Rapee, R.M., Dadds, M.M. and Ryan, S.M. (1996b). Family enhancement of cognitive style in anxious and aggressive children. *Journal of Abnormal Child Psychology*, *24*, 187–203.

Barrett, P., Shortt, A. and Healy, L. (2002). Do parent and child behaviours differentiate families whose children have obsessive-compulsive disorder from other clinic and non-clinic families? *Journal of Child Psychology and Psychiatry and Allied Disciplines*, *43*, 5, 597–607.

Barrett, P., Healy-Farrell, L. and March, J. (2004). Cognitive-behavioural family treatment of childhood obsessive-compulsive disorder: a controlled trial. *Journal of Academic Child and Adolescent Psychiatry*, *43*, 1, 46–62.

Baxter, L.R., Schwartz, J.M., Mazziotta, J.C., Phelps, M.E. and Pahl, J.J. (1988). Cerebral glucose metabolic rates in non-depressed obsessive-compulsives. *American Journal of Psychiatry*, *145*, 1560–1563.

Baxter, L.R., Schwartz, J.M., Bergam, K.S., Szuba, M.P., Guze, B.H., Mazziotta, J.C., *et al.* (1992). Caudate glucose metabolic rate changes with both drug and behaviour therapy for obsessive-compulsive disorder. *Archives of General Psychiatry*, *49*, 681–689.

Beck, A.T., Rush, A.J., Shaw, B.F. and Emery, G. (1979). *Cognitive therapy of depression*. New York: Guilford Press.

Berg, C.Z., Whitaker, A., Davies, M., Flament, M.F., *et al.* (1988). The survey form of the Leyton obsessional inventory – child version. *Journal of the American Academy of Child and Adolescent Psychiatry*, *27*, 6, 759–763.

Black, D.W., Gaffney, G.R., Schlosser, S. and Gabel, J. (2003). Children of parents with obsessive-compulsive disorder – a 2-year follow-up study. *Acta Psychiatrica Scandinavica*, *107*, 4, 305–313.

Bodden, D.H.M., Bogels, S.M., Nauta, M.H., de Haan, E., Ringrose, J., Appelboom, C., *et al.* (in press). Efficacy of individual versus family cognitive behavioural therapy in clinically anxious youth.

Bolton, D. and Perrin, S. (2008). Evaluation of exposure with response-prevention for obsessive compulsive disorder in childhood and adolescence. *Journal of Behavior Therapy and Experimental Psychiatry*, *39*, 1, 1–22.

Bolton, D., Luckie, M. and Steinberg, D. (1995). Long-term course of obsessive-compulsive disorder treated in adolescence. *Journal of the American Academy of Child and Adolescent Psychiatry*, *34*, 1441–1450.

Bolton, D., Dearsley, P., Madronal-Luque, R. and Baron-Cohen, S. (2002). Magical thinking in childhood and adolescence: development and relation to obsessive compulsion. *British Journal of Developmental Psychology*, *20*, 479–494.

Boone, K., Ananth, J., Philpott, L., Kaur, A. and Djenderedjian, A. (1991). Neuropsychological characteristics of nondepressed adults with obsessive compulsive disorder. *Neuropsychiatry, Neuropsychology and Behavioural Neurology*, *4*, 96–109.

Calvocoressi, L., Lewis, B., Harris, M., Trufan, S. J., Goodman, W.K., McDougle, C.J., *et al.* (1995) Family accommodation in obsessive-compulsive disorder. *American Journal of Psychiatry*, *152*, 441–443.

Carey, G. and Gottesman, I.I. (1981). Twin and family studies of anxiety, phobic and obsessive disorders. In D.F. Klein and J. Rabkin (eds) *Anxiety: New research and changing concepts*. New York: Raven Press.

Caron, C. and Rutter, M. (1991). Co-morbidity in child psychopathology: concepts, issues and research strategies. *Journal of Child Psychology and Psychiatry*, *32*, 1063–1080.

Carr, A. (1999). *Child and adolescent clinical psychology: a contextual approach.* New York: Routledge.

Cartwright-Hatton S., Roberts, C., Chitsabesan, P., Fothergill, C. and Harrington, R. (2004). Systematic review of the efficacy of cognitive behaviour therapies for childhood and adolescent anxiety disorders. *British Journal of Clinical Psychology*, *43*, 4, 421–436.

Chalfant, A.M., Rapee, R. and Carroll, L. (2007). Treating anxiety disorders in children with high functioning autism spectrum disorders: a controlled trial. *Journal of Autism and Developmental Disorders*, *37*, 10, 1842–1857.

Challacombe, F. and Salkovskis, P.M. (submitted). Aspects of parenting in mothers with OCD.

Chambers, W., Puig-Antich, J., Hirsch, M., *et al.* (1985). The assessment of affective disorders in children and adolescents by semi-structured interview: test–retest reliability of the schedule for affective disorders and schizophrenia for school-aged children. Present episode version. *Archives of General Psychiatry*, *42*, 696–702.

Christensen, K., Kim, S.W., Dyksen, M.W. and Hoover, K.M. (1992). Neuropsychological performance in obsessive compulsive disorder. *Biological Psychiatry*, *31*, 4–18.

Christenson, G.A. and Mackenzie, T.B. (1994). Trichotillomania. In M. Hersen and R.T. Ammerman (eds) *Handbook of prescriptive treatments for adults* (pp. 217–235). New York: Plenum.

Clark, D.A. (2004). *Cognitive-behavioural therapy for OCD.* New York: Guilford Press.

Clark, D.M. and Beck, A.T. (1988). Cognitive approaches. In C. Last and M. Hersen (eds) *Handbook of anxiety disorders* (pp. 362–385). New York: Pergamon.

Cobham, V.E., Dadds, M.R. and Spence, S.H. (1998). The role of parental anxiety in the treatment of childhood anxiety. *Journal of Consulting and Clinical Psychology*, *66*, 893–905.

Coleman, J.C. and Hendry, L.B. (1999). *The nature of adolescence.* London: Routledge.

Comer, J.S., Kendall, P.C., Franklin, M.E., Hudson, J.L. and Pimentel, S.S. (2004). Obsessing/worrying about the overlap between obsessive–compulsive disorder and generalised anxiety disorder in youth. *Clinical Psychology Review*, *24*, 6, 663–683.

Cougle, J.R., Salkovskis, P.M. and Thorpe, S.J. (in press). Reality-monitoring in obsessive-compulsive checkers using semi-idiographic stimuli. *Journal of Anxiety Disorders.*

Creswell, C. and Cartwright-Hatton, S. (2007). Family treatment of child anxiety: outcomes, limitations and future directions. *Clinical Child and Family Review*, *10*, 3, 232–252.

Crick, N. and Dodge, K.A. (1994). A review and reformulation of social information processing mechanisms in children's social adjustment. *Psychological Bulletin*, *115*, 74–101.

de Haan, E., Hoogduin, K., Buitelaar, J. and Keijsers, G. (1998). Behaviour therapy versus clomipramine for treatment of obsessive-compulsive disorder in children and adolescents. *Journal of the American Academy of Child and Adolescent Psychiatry*, *37*, 1022–1029.

Derisley, J., Libby, S., Clark, S. and Reynolds, S. (2005). Mental health, coping and family-functioning in parents of young people with obsessive-compulsive disorder and with anxiety disorders. *British Journal of Clinical Psychology*, *44*, 439–444.

Doherr, L., Reynolds, S., Wetherly, J. and Evans, E.H. (2005). Young children's ability to engage in cognitive therapy tasks: associations with age and educational experience. *Behavioural and Cognitive Psychotherapy*, *33*, 201–215.

Eley, T.C., Bolton, D., O'Connor, T.G., Perrin, S., Smith, P. and Plomin, R. (2003). A twin study of anxiety-related behaviours in pre-school children. *Journal of Child Psychology and Psychiatry and Allied Disciplines*, *44*, 7, 945–960.

Evans, D.W., Leckman, J.F., Carter, A., Reznick, J.S., Henshaw, D., King R.A., *et al.* (1997). Rituals, habit and perfectionism: the prevalence and development of compulsive-like behaviour in normal young children. *Child Development*, *68*, 58–68.

Fairburn, C.G., Cooper, Z. and Shafran, R. (2003). Cognitive behaviour therapy for eating disorders: a 'transdiagnostic' theory and treatment. *Behaviour Research and Therapy*, *41*, 5, 509–528.

Fiske, A.P. and Haslam, N. (1997). Is obsessive-compulsive disorder a pathology of the human disposition to perform socially meaningful rituals? Evidence of similar content. *Journal of Nervous and Mental Disease*, *185*, 4, 211–222.

Flament, M.F., Rapoport, J.L., Berg, C.J. and Sceery, W. (1985). Clomipramine treatment of childhood obsessive-compulsive disorder. *Archives of General Psychiatry*, *42*, 977–983.

Flament, M.F., Whitaker, A., Rapoport, J.L., Davies, M., Berg, C.J., Kalikow, K., *et al.* (1988). Obsessive compulsive disorder in adolescence: an epidemiological study. *Journal of the American Academy of Child and Adolescent Psychiatry*, *27*, 764–771.

Flavell, J.H., Flavell, E.R and Green, F.L. (2001). Developments of children's understanding of connections between thinking and feeling. *Psychological Science*, *12*, 430–432.

Foa, E., Kozak, M., Salkovskis, P., Cols, M. and Amir, N. (1998). The validation of a new obsessive compulsive disorder scale: the obsessive-compulsive inventory. *Psychological Assessment*, *10*, 3, 206–214.

Franklin, M.E., Kozak, M.J., Cashman, L., Coles, M., Rheingold, A. and Foa, E.B. (1998). Cognitive-behavioural treatment of pediatric obsessive-compulsive disorder: an open clinical trial. *Journal of the American Academy of Child and Adolescent Psychiatry*, *37*, 412–419.

Freeston, M.H., Ladouceur, R., Gagnon, F., Thibodeau, N., Rheame, J., Letarte, H., *et al.* (1997). Cognitive-behavioural treatment of obsessive thoughts: a controlled study. *Journal of Consulting and Clinical Psychology*, *65*, 405–413.

Geller, D.A., Biederman, J., Jones, J., Shapiro, S., Schwartz, S. and Park, K.S. (1998). Obsessive-compulsive disorder in children and adolescents: a review. *Harvard Review of Psychiatry*, *5*, 5, 260–273.

Geller, D., Biederman, J., Faraone, S., Agranat, A., Cradlock, K. and Hagermoser, L. (2001). Developmental aspects of obsessive-compulsive disorder: findings in children, adolescents and adults. *Journal of Nervous and Mental Disease*, *189*, 471–477.

Geller, D.A., Biederman, J., Stewart, S.E., Mullin, B., Martin, A., Spencer, T., *et al.* (2003). Which SSRI? A meta-analysis of pharmacotherapy trials in pediatric obsessive-compulsive disorder. *American Journal of Psychiatry*, *160*, 1919–1928.

Goodman, R., Ford, T., Richards, H., Gatward, R. and Meltzer, H. (2000). The development and well-being assessment: description and initial validation of an integrated assessment of child and adolescent psychopathology. *Journal of Child Psychology and Psychiatry*, *41*, 5, 645–655.

Goodman, W.K., Price, L.H., Rasmussan, S.A., Mazure, C., Fleischmann, R.L.,

Hill, C. L., *et al.* (1989). The Yale-Brown obsessive-compulsive scale I. Development, use and reliability. *Archives of General Psychiatry*, *46*, 1006–1011.

Grave, J. and Blissett, J. (2005). Is cognitive behaviour therapy developmentally appropriate for young children? A critical review of the evidence. *Clinical Psychology Review*, *24*, 4, 399–420.

Greenberger, D. and Padesky, C.A. (1995). *Mind over mood: a cognitive therapy treatment manual for clients.* New York: Guilford Press.

Griffen, N. (2000). Inflated responsibility and obsessionality in adolescents. Submitted in part fulfilment of the degree of MSc in research methods in psychology, University of Reading.

Grotevant, H.D. and Cooper, C.R. (1986). Individuation in family relationships: a perspective on individual differences in the development of identity. *Human Development*, *29*, 82–100.

Hanna, G.L. (1995). Demographic and clinical features of obsessive-compulsive disorder in children and adolescents. *Journal of the American Academy of Child and Adolescent Psychiatry*, *34*, 19–27.

Hanna, G.L., Piacentini, J., Cantwell, D.P., Fischer, D.J., Himle, J.A. and Van Etten, M. (2002). Obsessive-compulsive disorder with and without tics in a clinical sample of children and adolescents. *Depression and Anxiety*, *16*, 2, 59–63.

Hanna, G.L., Himle, J.A., Curtis, G.C. and Gillespie, B.W. (2005). A family study of obsessive-compulsive disorder with pediatric probands. *American Journal of Medical Genetics Part B: Neuropsychiatric Genetics*, *134B*, 1, 13–19.

Hartl, T.L. and Frost, R.O. (1999). Cognitive-behavioural treatment of compulsive hoarding: a multiple baseline experimental case study. *Behaviour Research and Therapy*, *37*, 5, 451–461.

Head, D., Bolton, D. and Hymas, N. (1989). Deficit in cognitive shifting ability in patients with obsessive-compulsive disorder. *Biological Psychiatry*, *25*, 929–937.

Herjanic, B. and Reich, W. (1982). Development of a structured psychiatric interview for children: agreement between child and parent on individual symptoms. *Journal of Abnormal Child Psychology*, *10*, 307–324.

Heyman, I., Fombonne, E., Simmons, H., Ford, T., Meltzer, H. and Goodman, R. (2001). Prevalence of obsessive-compulsive disorder in the British nationwide survey of child mental health. *British Journal of Psychiatry*, *179*, 324–329.

Hibbs, E., Hamburger, S., Lenane, M., *et al.* (1991). Determinants of expressed emotion in families of disturbed and normal children. *Journal of Child Psychology and Psychiatry*, *32*, 757–770.

Hodgson, R.J. and Rachman, J. (1977). Obsessive-compulsive complaints. *Behaviour Research and Therapy*, *15*, 5, 389–395.

Hollander, E. (1997). Obsessive-compulsive disorder: the hidden epidemic. *Journal of Clinical Psychiatry*, *58*, 12, 3–6.

Insel, T.R., Mueller, E.A., Alterman, I., Linnoila, M. and Murphy, D.L. (1985). Obsessive-compulsive disorder and serotonin: is there a connection? *Biological Psychiatry*, *20*, 1174–1185.

Karno, M., Golding, J.M., Sorenson, S.B. and Burnam, A. (1988). The epidemiology of obsessive-compulsive disorder in five US communities. *Archives of General Psychiatry*, *45*, 1094–1099.

Kaufman, J., Birmaher, B., Brent, D., Rao, U. Flynn, C., Moreci, P., *et al.* (1997). Schedule for affective disorders and schizophrenia for school-age children – present and lifetime version (K-SADS-PL): initial reliability and validity data. *Journal of the American Academy of Child and Adolescent Psychiatry*, *36*, 7, 980–988.

Kovacs, M. (1992). *The children's depression inventory manual*. Toronto: Multi-Health Systems.

Kovas, Y. and Plomin, R. (2006). Generalist genes: implications for the cognitive sciences. *Trends in Cognitive Sciences*, *10*, 5, 198–203.

Lam, D.C. and Salkovskis, P.M. (2007). An experimental investigation of the impact of biological and psychological causal explanations on anxious and depressed patients' perception of a person with panic disorder. *Behaviour Research and Therapy*, *45*, 2, 405–411.

Lam, D.C.K., Salkovskis, P.M. and Warwick, H.M.C. (2005). An experimental investigation of the impact of biological versus psychological explanations of the cause of 'mental illness'. *Journal of Mental Health*, *14*, 5, 453–464.

Lam, D.C.K., Poplavskaya, E.V. and Salkovskis, P.M. (submitted). An experimental investigation of the impact of personality disorder diagnosis on clinicians: can we see past the borderline?

Leckman, J.F. (1993). Tourette's syndrome. In E. Hollander (ed.) *Obsessive-compulsive related disorders* (pp. 113–138). Washington, DC: American Psychiatric Press.

Leckman, J.F., Grice, D.E., Barr, L.C., de Vries, A.L.C., Martin, C., Cohen, D.J. *et al.* (1995). Tic-related versus non-tic related obsessive compulsive disorder. *Anxiety*, *1*, 208–215.

Lehmkuhl, H.D., Storch, E.A., Bodfish, J.W. and Geffken, G.R. (2007). Brief report: exposure and response prevention for obsessive compulsive disorder in a 12-year-old with autism. *Journal of Autism Developmental Disorders* (e-publication).

Lensi, P., Cassano, G.B., Correddu, G., Ravagli, S., Kunovac, J.L. and Akiskal, H.S. (1996). Obsessive-compulsive disorder: familial-developmental history, symptomatology, co-morbidity and course with special reference to gender-related differences. *British Journal of Psychiatry*, *169*, 101–107.

Leonard, H.L., Swedo, S.E., Rapoport, J.L., Koby, E.V., Lenane, M.C., Cheslow, D.L., *et al.* (1989). Treatment of childhood obsessive-compulsive disorder with clomipramine and desipramine: a double-blind crossover comparison. *Archives of General Psychiatry*, *46*, 1088–1092.

Libby, S., Reynolds, S., Derisley, J. and Clark, S. (2004). Cognitive appraisals in young people with obsessive-compulsive disorder. *Journal of Child Psychology and Psychiatry*, *45*, 6, 1076–1084.

McKeon, J., Roa, B. and Mann, A. (1984). Life events and personality traits in obsessive-compulsive neurosis. *British Journal of Psychiatry*, *144*, 185–189.

MacDonald, A.M., Murray, R.M. and Clifford, C.A. (1992). The contribution of heredity to obsessional disorder and personality: a review of family and twin study evidence. In M.T. Tsuang, K.S. Viendler and M.J. Lyons (Eds) *Genetic issues in psychosocial epidemiology*. New Brunswick: Rutgers University Press.

MacFarlane, M.M. (2001). Systemic treatment of obsessive-compulsive disorder in a rural community mental health centre: an integrative approach. In M.M. MacFarlane (ed.) *Family therapy and mental health: innovations in theory and practice* (pp. 155–183). New York: Haworth Clinical Practice Press.

March, J.S. (1997). *Manual for the multi-dimensional anxiety scale for children (MASC)*. Toronto: Multi-Health Systems.

March, J.S. and Mulle, K. (1998). *Obsessive compulsive disorder in children and adolescents: a cognitive-behavioural treatment manual*. New York: Guilford Press.

March, J.S., Frances, A., Kahn, D.A. and Carpenter, D. (eds) (1997). The expert consensus guideline series: treatment of obsessive-compulsive disorder. *Journal of Clinical Psychiatry*, *58* (suppl. 4).

March, J.S., Foa., E., Gammon, P., Chrisman, A., Curry, J., Fitzgerald, D., *et al.* (2004). Cognitive-behaviour therapy, sertraline and their combination for children and adolescents with obsessive-compulsive disorder. The Pediatric OCD treatment study (POTS) randomised controlled trial. *Journal of the American Medical Association*, *292*, 1969–1976.

Marks, I. (1987). *Fears, phobias and rituals: panic, anxiety and their disorders.* Oxford: Oxford University Press.

Mell, L.K., Davis, R.L. and Owens, D. (2005). Association between streptococcal infection and obsessive-compulsive disorder, Tourette's syndrome and tic disorder. *Pediatrics*, *116*, 1, 56–60.

Merlo, L.J., Storch, E.A., Murphy, T.K., Goodman, W.K. and Geffken, G.R. (2005). Assessment of paediatric obsessive-compulsive disorder: a critical review of current methodology. *Child Psychiatry and Human Development*, *36*, 2, 195–214.

Meyer, V. (1966). Modifications of expectations in cases with obsessional rituals. *Behaviour Research and Therapy*, *4*, 273–280.

Meyer, V., Levy, R. and Schnurer, A. (1974). The behavioural treatment of obsessive compulsive disorders. In H.R. Beech (ed.) *Obsessional states* (pp. 233–258). London: Methuen.

Mowrer, O.H. (1960). *Learning theory and behaviour.* New York: Wiley.

Muris, P., Merckelbach, H. and Clavan, M. (1997). Abnormal and normal compulsions. *Behaviour Research and Therapy*, *35*, 249–252.

Muris, P., Merckelbach, H., Van Brakel, A. and Mayer, B. (1999). The revised version of the screen for child anxiety related emotional disorders (SCARED-R): further evidence for its reliability and validity. *Anxiety, Stress, and Coping*, *12*, 4, 411–425.

Muris, P., Meesters, C., Rassin, E., Merckelbach, H. and Campbell, J. (2001). Thought–action fusion and anxiety disorders symptoms in normal adolescents. *Behaviour Research and Therapy*, *39*, 7, 843–852.

National Institute for Health and Clinical Excellence (NICE, 2005). *Obsessive compulsive disorder: core interventions in the treatment of obsessive compulsive disorder and body dysmorphic disorder. Guideline 31.* London: British Psychological Society and the Royal College of Psychiatrists.

Obsessive Compulsive Cognitions Working Group (OCCWG, 1997). Cognitive assessment of obsessive-compulsive disorder. *Behaviour Research and Therapy*, *35*, 667–681.

O'Kearney, R.T., Anstey, K.J. and von Sanden, C. (2006). Behavioural and cognitive behavioural therapy for obsessive compulsive disorder in children and adolescents. *Cochrane Database of Systematic Reviews*, *4*, art. no.: CD004856. DOI: 10.1002/14651858.CD004856.pub2.

Pauls, D.L., Alsobrook, J.P., Goodman, W., Rasmussen, S. and Leckman, J.F. (1995). A family study of obsessive-compulsive disorder. *American Journal of Psychiatry*, *152*, 76–84.

Piacentini J. and Jaffer, M. (1999). *Measuring functional impairment in youngsters with OCD: manual for the child OCD impact scale (COIS).* Los Angeles: UCLA Department of Psychiatry.

Piacentini, J., Bergman, R.L., Keller, M. and McCracken, J. (2003). Functional impairment in children and adolescents with obsessive-compulsive disorder. *Journal of Child and Adolescent Psychopharmacology*, *13*, S61–S69.

Quakley, S., Coker, S., Palmer, K. and Reynolds, S. (2003). Can children distinguish between thoughts and behaviours? *Behavioural and Cognitive Psychotherapy*, *31*, 159–168.

Quakley, S., Reynolds, S. and Coker, S. (2004). The effect of cues on young children's abilities to discriminate among thoughts, feelings and behaviours. *Behaviour Research and Therapy*, *42*, 3, 343–356.

Rachman, S.J. (1971). Obsessional ruminations. *Behaviour Research and Therapy*, *9*, 229–235.

Rachman, S. (1983). Obstacles to the successful treatment of obsessions. In E.B. Foa and P.M.G. Emmelkamp (eds) *Failures in behavior therapy* (pp. 35–57). Toronto: Wiley.

Rachman, S.J. (1997). A cognitive theory of obsessions. *Behaviour Research and Therapy*, *35*, 9, 793–802.

Rachman, S.J. (1998). A cognitive theory of obsessions: elaborations. *Behaviour Research and Therapy*, *36*, 385–401.

Rachman, S.J. (2003). *The treatment of obsessions*. Oxford: Oxford University Press.

Rachman, S.J. and de Silva, P. (1978). Abnormal and normal obsessions. *Behaviour Research and Therapy*, *16*, 233–248.

Rachman, S. and Hodgson, R.J. (1980). *Obsessions and compulsions*. Englewood Cliffs, NJ: Prentice-Hall.

Rachman, S.J. and Shafran, R. (1998). Cognitive and behavioural features of obsessive-compulsive disorder. In R.P. Swinson, M.M. Antony, S. Rachman and M.A. Richter (eds) *Obsessive-compulsive disorder: theory, research and treatment* (pp. 51–78). New York: Guilford Press.

Rachman, S.J., Hodgson, R. and Marks, I.M. (1971). The treatment of chronic obsessive-compulsive neurosis. *Behaviour Research and Therapy*, *9*, 237–247.

Radomsky, A.S., Rachman, S. and Hammond, D. (2001). Memory bias, confidence and responsibility in compulsive checking. *Behaviour Research and Therapy*, *39*, 813–822.

Rapee, R.M. (2001). The development of generalised anxiety. In M.W. Vasey and M.M. Dadds (eds) *The developmental psychopathology of anxiety* (pp. 1045–1095). New York: Oxford University Press.

Rapoport, J. (1989). *The boy who couldn't stop washing*. London: Williams Collins.

Rapoport, J.L. and Inoff-Germain, G., (2000). Practitioner review: treatment of obsessive-compulsive disorder in children and adolescents. *Journal of Child Psychology and Psychiatry*, *41*, 4, 419–431.

Rasmussen, S.A. and Eisen, J.L. (1992). The epidemiology and clinical features of obsessive-compulsive disorder. *Psychiatric Clinics of North America*, *15*, 743–758.

Reaven, J. and Hepburn, S. (2003). Cognitive-behavioural treatment of obsessive-compulsive disorder in a child with Asperger syndrome: a case report. *Autism*, *7*, 2, 145–164.

Rector, N.A., Richter, M.A., Denisoff, E., Crawford, C., Bourdeau, D., Bradbury, C., *et al.* (2006). Exposure response prevention versus integrated CBT for refractory OCD: efficacy and predictors of outcome. Paper presented at the European Association of Behavioural and Cognitive Therapy Conference, Paris.

Rettew, D.C., Swedo, S.E., Leonard, H.L., Lenane, M.C. and Rapoport, J.L. (1992). Obsessions and compulsions across time in 79 children and adolescents with obsessive-compulsive disorder. *Journal of the American Academy of Child Adolescent Psychiatry*, *31*, 1050–1056.

Riddle, M.A., Scahill, L., King, R., Hardin, M.T., Towbin, K.E., Ort, S.I., *et al.* (1990). Obsessive compulsive disorder in children and adolescents: phenomenology and family history. *Journal of the American Academy of Child and Adolescent Psychiatry*, *5*, 766–772.

Rimes, K.A. and Salkovskis, P.M. (1998). Psychological effects of genetic testing for psychological disorders. *Behavioural and Cognitive Psychotherapy*, *26*, 29–42.

Robinson, E.J. and Beck, S.R. (2000). What is difficult about counterfactual reasoning? In P. Mitchell and K.J. Riggs (eds) *Children's reasoning and the mind*. Hove, UK: Psychology Press.

Rosenberg, M. (1979). *Conceiving the self*. New York: Basic Books.

Salkovskis, P.M. (1985). Obsessional-compulsive problems: a cognitive-behavioural analysis. *Behaviour Research and Therapy*, *23*, 571–583.

Salkovskis, P.M. (1996a). Cognitive-behavioural approaches to the understanding of obsessional problems. In R.M. Rapee (ed.) *Current controversies in the anxiety disorders* (pp. 191–200). New York: Guilford Press.

Salkovskis, P.M. (1996b). Understanding of obsessive-compulsive disorder is not improved by redefining it as something else: Reply to Pigott *et al.* and to Enright. In R.M. Rapee (ed.) *Current controversies in the anxiety disorders* (pp. 191–200). New York: Guilford Press.

Salkovskis, P.M. (1998). Psychological approaches to the understanding of obsessional problems. In R.P. Swinson, M.M. Antony, S. Rachman and M.A. Richter (eds) *Obsessive-compulsive disorder: theory, research and treatment* (pp. 33–50) New York: Guilford Press.

Salkovskis, P.M. and Harrison, J. (1984). Abnormal or normal obsessions: a replication. *Behaviour Research and Therapy*, *22*, 1–4.

Salkovskis, P.M. and Warwick, H.M.C. (1985). Cognitive therapy of obsessive-compulsive disorder: treating treatment failures. *Behavioural Psychotherapy*, *13*, 243–255.

Salkovskis, P. and Williams, T. (2004a). Child obsessive compulsive inventory (Child OCI). Unpublished manuscript.

Salkovskis, P. and Williams, T. (2004b). Child responsibility interpretations questionnaires (CRIQ) and child responsibility attitudes questionnaire (CRAS). Unpublished manuscript.

Salkovskis, P.M, Forrester, E., Richards, C. and Morrison, N. (1998). The devil is in the detail: conceptualising and treating obsessional problems. In N. Tarrier, A. Wells and G. Haddock (eds) *Treating complex cases: the cognitive behavioural therapy approach*. New York: Wiley.

Salkovskis, P.M., Shafran, R., Rachman, S. and Freeston, M.H. (1999). Multiple pathways to inflated responsibility beliefs in obsessional problems: possible origins and implications for therapy and research. *Behaviour Research and Therapy*, *37*, 1055–1072.

Salkovskis, P., Wroe, A., Gledhill, A., Morrison, N., Forrester, C., Richards, C., *et al.* (2000). Responsibility attitudes and interpretations are characteristic of obsessive compulsive disorder. *Behaviour Research and Therapy*, *38*, 347–372.

Salkovskis, P.M., Forrester, E., Richards, C., Deale, A., McGuire, J., Taylor, T., *et al.* (in press). Cognitive-behavioural therapy compared with behavioural therapy in obsessive compulsive disorder: a controlled trial. *British Journal of Psychiatry*.

Salmon, K. and Bryant, R. (2002). Posttraumatic stress disorder in children: a developmental perspective. *Clinical Psychology Review*, *22*, 163–188.

Scahill, L., Riddle, M., McSwiggin-Gardin, M., Ort, S.I., King, R.A., Goodman, W.K., *et al.* (1997). Children's Yale Brown Obsessive Compulsive Scale: reliability and validity. *Journal of the American Academy of Child and Adolescent Psychiatry*, *36*, 844–852.

Shafran, R. (2001). Obsessive-compulsive disorder in children and adolescents. *Child Psychology and Psychiatry Review*, *6*, 2, 50–58.

Shafran, R., Frampton, I., Heyman, I., Reynolds, M., Teachman, B. and Rachman, S. (2003). The preliminary development of a new self-report measure for OCD in young people. *Journal of Adolescence, 26*, 137–142.

Shear, K.A., Jin, R., Ruscio, A.M., Walters, E.E. and Kessler, R.C. (2006). Prevalence and correlates of estimated DSM-IV child and adult separation anxiety disorder in the national co-morbidity survey replication. *American Journal of Psychiatry, 163*, 1074–1083.

Silverman, W.K. and Albano, A.M. (1996). *The anxiety disorders interview schedule for DSM-IV: child and parent versions.* San Antonio, TX: Graywind.

Skoog, G. and Skoog, I. (1999). A 40-year follow-up of patients with obsessive-compulsive disorder. *Archives of General Psychiatry, 56*, 121–127.

Snider, L.A. and Swedo, S.E. (2004). PANDAS: current status and directions for research. *Molecular Psychiatry, 9*, 900–907.

Sofronoff, K., Attwood, T. and Hinton, S. (2005). A randomised controlled trial of a CBT intervention for anxiety in children with Asperger syndrome. *Journal of Child Psychology and Psychiatry and Allied Disciplines, 46*, 11, 1152–1160.

Stallard, P. (2005). Cognitive behaviour therapy with pre-pubertal children. In P.J. Graham (ed.) *Cognitive behaviour therapy for children and families*, 2nd edn. London: University College and Institute of Child Health.

Stewart, S.E., Geller, D.A., Jenike, M., Pauls, D., Shaw, D., Mullin, B., *et al.* (2004). Long-term outcome of pediatric obsessive-compulsive disorder: a meta-analysis and qualitative review of the literature. *Acta Psychiatrica Scandinavica, 110*, 4–13.

Stobie, B., Taylor, T., Quigley, A., Ewing, S. and Salkovskis, P.M. (2007). 'Contents may vary': a pilot study of treatment histories of OCD patients. *Cognitive and Behavioural Psychotherapy, 35*, 3, 273–282.

Swedo, S.E. and Rapoport, J.L. (1989). Phenomenology and differential diagnosis of obsessive-compulsive disorder in children and adolescents. In J.L. Rapoport (ed.) *Obsessive compulsive disorder in children and adolescents*. Washington, DC: American Psychiatric Press.

Swedo, S.E., Leonard, H.L., Rapoport, J.L., Lenane, M.C., Goldberger, E.L. and Cheslow, D.L. (1989a). A double-blind comparison of clomipramine and desipramine in the treatment of trichotillomania (hair pulling). *New England Journal of Medicine, 321*, 497–501.

Swedo, S.E., Rapoport, J.L., Leonard, H., Lenane, M. and Cheslow, D. (1989b). Obsessive compulsive disorder in children and adolescents. Clinical phenomenology of 70 consecutive cases. *Archives of General Psychiatry, 46*, 335–341.

Swedo, S.E., Leonard, H.L., Garvey, M., Mittleman, B., Allen, A.J., Perlmutter, S.J., *et al.* (1998). Pediatric autoimmune disorders associated with streptococcal infections: clinical description of the first 50 cases. *American Journal of Psychiatry, 155*, 2, 264–271.

Sze, K.M. and Wood, J.J. (2007) Cognitive behavioral treatment of comorbid anxiety disorders and social difficulties in children with high-functioning autism: a case report. *Journal of Contemporary Psychotherapy, 37*, 3, 133.

Thelen, E. (1981). Kicking, rocking, and waving: contextual analysis of rhythmical stereotypes in normal human infants. *Animal Behaviour, 29*, 3–11.

Thomsen, P.H. (1999). *From thoughts to obsessions: obsessive compulsive disorders in children and adolescents*, D. Christophersen, trans. London: Jessica Kingsley Publishers.

Thomsen, P.H. and Mikkelson, H.U. (1995). Course of obsessive-compulsive disorder in children and adolescents: a prospective Danish study of 23 Danish cases.

Journal of the American Academy of Child and Adolescent Psychiatry, *34*, 1432–1440.

Tolin, D.F. (2001). Case study: bibliotherapy and extinction treatment of obsessive-compulsive disorder in a 5-year-old boy. *Journal of the American Academy of Child and Adolescent Psychiatry*, *40*, 9, 1111–1114.

Tomm, K. (1988). Interventive interviewing: III. Intending to ask lineal, circular, strategic, or reflexive questions? *Family Process*, *27*, 1–15.

Torres, A.R., Prince, M.J., Bebbington, P.E., Bhugra, D.K., Brugha, T.S., Farrell, M., *et al.* (2007). Treatment seeking by individuals with obsessive-compulsive disorder from the British Psychiatric Morbidity Survey of 2000. *Psychiatric Services*, *58*, 977–982.

Troster, H. (1994). Prevalence and functions of stereotyped behaviors in nonhandicapped children in residential care. *Journal of Abnormal Child Psychology 22*, 79–97.

Valleni-Basile, L.A., Garrison, C.Z., Jackson, K.L., Waller, J.L., McKeown, R.E., Addy, C.L., *et al.* (1995). Family and psychosocial predictors of obsessive compulsive disorder in a community sample of young adolescents. *Journal of Child and Family Studies*, *4*, 193–206.

Wagner, A. P. (2006). *What to do when your child has obsessive-compulsive disorder: strategies and solutions*. Rochester, NY: Lighthouse Press.

Wellman, H.M., Hollander, M. and Schult, C.A. (1996). Young children's understanding of thought bubbles and thoughts. *Child Development*, *67*, 768–788.

Wever, C. and Rey, J.M. (1997). Juvenile obsessive-compulsive disorder. *Australian and New Zealand Journal of Psychiatry*, *31*, 1, 105–113.

Wewetzer, C., Jans, T., Muller, B., Neudorfl, A., Bucherl, U., Remschmidt, H., *et al.* (2001). Long-term outcome and prognosis of obsessive-compulsive disorder with onset in childhood or adolescence. *European Child and Adolescent Psychiatry*, *10*, 1, 37–46.

Williams, T.I., Salkovskis, P.M., Forrester, E.A. and Allsopp, M.A. (2002). Changes in symptoms of OCD and appraisal of responsibility during cognitive behavioural treatment: a pilot study. *Behavioural and Cognitive Psychotherapy*, *30*, 69–78.

Wolff, R.D. and Wolff, R. (1991). Assessment and treatment of obsessive-compulsive disorder in children. *Behaviour Modification*, *15*, 3, 372–393.

Zohar, A.H. (1999). The epidemiology of obsessive-compulsive disorder in children and adolescents. *Child and Adolescent Psychiatric Clinics of North America*, *8*, 445–460.

Zohar, J., Insel, T.R., Zohar-Kadouch, R.C., Hill, J.L. and Murphy, D.L. (1988). Serotonergic responsivity in obsessive-compulsive disorder: effects of chronic clomipramine treatment. *Archives of General Psychiatry*, *45*, 167–172.

Appendix A

Child Obsessive Compulsive Inventory (Child OCI)

The following statements are about things that happen to many people in their everyday lives. For each statement, draw a circle around the number which says best how much it has troubled you in the **last week**.

0 = has not troubled me at all
1 = troubled me a little
2 = definitely troubled me
3 = troubled me a lot
4 = troubled me extremely

		Not at all	A little	Definitely	A lot	Extremely
1	Bad thoughts come into my mind even if I don't want them to, and I can't get rid of them.	0	1	2	3	4
2	If I touch or if I'm near sweat, saliva, blood, or urine I might get germs on my clothes or somehow be harmed.	0	1	2	3	4
3	I ask people to repeat things to me many times, even though I knew what they meant the first time.	0	1	2	3	4
4	I have to wash and clean all the time.	0	1	2	3	4

	Not at all	A little	Definitely	A lot	Extremely
5 I have to think through things that happened in the past to make sure that I didn't do something wrong.	0	1	2	3	4
6 I have saved up so many things that they get in the way.	0	1	2	3	4
7 I check things more often than I need to.	0	1	2	3	4
8 I try not to use public toilets because I am afraid of disease or germs.	0	1	2	3	4
9 I check doors, windows, drawers, etc. over and over.	0	1	2	3	4
10 I check water taps and light switches over and over after turning them off.	0	1	2	3	4
11 I collect things I don't need.	0	1	2	3	4
12 I sometimes think I might have hurt someone without knowing it.	0	1	2	3	4
13 I have thoughts that I might want to hurt myself or others.	0	1	2	3	4
14 I get upset if things are not arranged properly.	0	1	2	3	4
15 I have to follow a certain order in dressing, undressing and washing myself.	0	1	2	3	4
16 I feel I have to count while I am doing things.	0	1	2	3	4
17 I am afraid of doing embarrassing or harmful things on impulse.	0	1	2	3	4

18	I need to pray to stop bad thoughts or feelings.	0	1	2	3	4
19	I keep on checking homework or other things I have written.	0	1	2	3	4
20	I get upset at the sight of knives, scissors and other sharp objects in case I lose control with them.	0	1	2	3	4
21	I am concerned too much about being clean.	0	1	2	3	4
22	I find it hard to touch an object when I know it has been touched by strangers or certain people.	0	1	2	3	4
23	I need things to be arranged in a certain order.	0	1	2	3	4
24	I get behind in my schoolwork because I do the same things over and over again.	0	1	2	3	4
25	I feel I have to repeat certain numbers.	0	1	2	3	4
26	After doing something carefully, I still feel I have not finished it.	0	1	2	3	4
27	I find it hard to touch rubbish or dirty things.	0	1	2	3	4
28	I find it hard to control my own thoughts.	0	1	2	3	4
29	I have to do things over and over again until it feels right.	0	1	2	3	4
30	I am upset by bad thoughts that come into my mind even though I don't want them to.	0	1	2	3	4

		Not at all	A little	Definitely	A lot	Extremely
31	Before going to sleep I have to do certain things in a certain way.	0	1	2	3	4
32	I go back to places to make sure that I have not harmed anyone.	0	1	2	3	4
33	I often get nasty thoughts and it's hard to get rid of them.	0	1	2	3	4
34	I try not to throw things away because I am afraid I might need them later.	0	1	2	3	4
35	I get upset if others change the way I have arranged my things.	0	1	2	3	4
36	I feel that I must repeat certain words or phrases in my mind to wipe out bad thoughts, bad feelings or bad things I do.	0	1	2	3	4
37	After I have done things, I'm never quite sure whether I really did them.	0	1	2	3	4
38	I sometimes have to wash or clean myself just because I feel have germs.	0	1	2	3	4
39	I feel that there are good and bad numbers.	0	1	2	3	4
40	I check anything which could go on fire over and over.	0	1	2	3	4
41	Even when I do something very carefully I feel that it is not quite right.	0	1	2	3	4
42	I wash my hands more often or longer than I need to.	0	1	2	3	4

W	C	D	O	Ob	H	N
☐	☐	☐	☐	☐	☐	☐

Total

☐

Instructions for scoring the Child Obsessive Compulsive Inventory

- Add together the scores for questions 2, 4, 8, 16, 21, 22, 27, 38, 42 to obtain the score for Washing subscale (box labelled W).
- Add together the scores for questions 3, 7, 9, 10, 19, 24, 32, 40 to obtain the score for the Checking subscale (box labelled C)
- Add together the scores for questions 26, 37, 41 to obtain the score for the Doubting subscale (box labelled D)
- Add together the scores for questions 14, 15, 23, 29, 31, 35 to obtain the score for the Ordering subscale (box labelled O)
- Add together the scores for questions 1, 12, 13, 17, 20, 28, 30 to obtain the score for the Obsessionality subscale (box labelled Ob)
- Add together the scores for questions 6, 11, 34 to obtain the score for the Hoarding subscale (box labelled H)
- Add together the scores for questions 5, 18, 25 to obtain the score for the Neutralising subscale (box labelled N)
- Add all the above scores to generate the total score for the OCI.

Appendix B

Child Responsibility Attitude Scale (CRAS)

This questionnaire lists beliefs which people sometimes have. Read each statement carefully and decide how much you agree or disagree with it. For each of the beliefs, put a circle round the words which **best describe how you think**. Choose only one answer for each attitude. Because people are different, there are no right or wrong answers. To decide whether a given attitude is like your way of looking at things, simply keep in mind what you are like **most of the time**.

1 I often feel responsible for things that go wrong.

TOTALLY AGREE	AGREE VERY MUCH	AGREE SLIGHTLY	NEUTRAL	DISAGREE SLIGHTLY	DISAGREE VERY MUCH	TOTALLY DISAGREE

2 If I think bad things, this is as bad as *doing* bad things.

TOTALLY AGREE	AGREE VERY MUCH	AGREE SLIGHTLY	NEUTRAL	DISAGREE SLIGHTLY	DISAGREE VERY MUCH	TOTALLY DISAGREE

3 I worry a lot about what might happen because of things that I do or don't do.

TOTALLY AGREE	AGREE VERY MUCH	AGREE SLIGHTLY	NEUTRAL	DISAGREE SLIGHTLY	DISAGREE VERY MUCH	TOTALLY DISAGREE

4 Not stopping bad things happening is as bad as making them happen.

TOTALLY AGREE	AGREE VERY MUCH	AGREE SLIGHTLY	NEUTRAL	DISAGREE SLIGHTLY	DISAGREE VERY MUCH	TOTALLY DISAGREE

5 I should always try to stop harm happening when I have thought it might.

TOTALLY AGREE	AGREE VERY MUCH	AGREE SLIGHTLY	NEUTRAL	DISAGREE SLIGHTLY	DISAGREE VERY MUCH	TOTALLY DISAGREE

6 I must always think through what might happen as a result of even the smallest things I do.

TOTALLY AGREE	AGREE VERY MUCH	AGREE SLIGHTLY	NEUTRAL	DISAGREE SLIGHTLY	DISAGREE VERY MUCH	TOTALLY DISAGREE

7 I often take responsibility for things which other people don't think are my fault.

TOTALLY AGREE	AGREE VERY MUCH	AGREE SLIGHTLY	NEUTRAL	DISAGREE SLIGHTLY	DISAGREE VERY MUCH	TOTALLY DISAGREE

8 Everything I do can cause serious problems.

TOTALLY AGREE	AGREE VERY MUCH	AGREE SLIGHTLY	NEUTRAL	DISAGREE SLIGHTLY	DISAGREE VERY MUCH	TOTALLY DISAGREE

9　I often nearly cause harm.

TOTALLY AGREE	AGREE VERY MUCH	AGREE SLIGHTLY	NEUTRAL	DISAGREE SLIGHTLY	DISAGREE VERY MUCH	TOTALLY DISAGREE

10　I must protect others from harm.

TOTALLY AGREE	AGREE VERY MUCH	AGREE SLIGHTLY	NEUTRAL	DISAGREE SLIGHTLY	DISAGREE VERY MUCH	TOTALLY DISAGREE

11　I should never cause even the smallest amount of harm to others.

TOTALLY AGREE	AGREE VERY MUCH	AGREE SLIGHTLY	NEUTRAL	DISAGREE SLIGHTLY	DISAGREE VERY MUCH	TOTALLY DISAGREE

12　I will be condemned for my actions.

TOTALLY AGREE	AGREE VERY MUCH	AGREE SLIGHTLY	NEUTRAL	DISAGREE SLIGHTLY	DISAGREE VERY MUCH	TOTALLY DISAGREE

13　I must try to stop bad things from happening, if there is any chance that what I do might make a difference.

TOTALLY AGREE	AGREE VERY MUCH	AGREE SLIGHTLY	NEUTRAL	DISAGREE SLIGHTLY	DISAGREE VERY MUCH	TOTALLY DISAGREE

14　Doing nothing when bad things might happen is the same as making it happen.

TOTALLY AGREE	AGREE VERY MUCH	AGREE SLIGHTLY	NEUTRAL	DISAGREE SLIGHTLY	DISAGREE VERY MUCH	TOTALLY DISAGREE

15　You should never be careless, when what you do might affect someone else.

TOTALLY AGREE	AGREE VERY MUCH	AGREE SLIGHTLY	NEUTRAL	DISAGREE SLIGHTLY	DISAGREE VERY MUCH	TOTALLY DISAGREE

16　If I do nothing that can cause as much harm as doing something bad.

TOTALLY AGREE	AGREE VERY MUCH	AGREE SLIGHTLY	NEUTRAL	DISAGREE SLIGHTLY	DISAGREE VERY MUCH	TOTALLY DISAGREE

17 I can't forgive myself, once I think it is possible that I have caused harm.

TOTALLY AGREE | AGREE VERY MUCH | AGREE SLIGHTLY | NEUTRAL | DISAGREE SLIGHTLY | DISAGREE VERY MUCH | TOTALLY DISAGREE

18 Lots of things I have done have been meant to prevent harm to others.

TOTALLY AGREE | AGREE VERY MUCH | AGREE SLIGHTLY | NEUTRAL | DISAGREE SLIGHTLY | DISAGREE VERY MUCH | TOTALLY DISAGREE

19 If I am careful enough then I can prevent any harmful accidents.

TOTALLY AGREE | AGREE VERY MUCH | AGREE SLIGHTLY | NEUTRAL | DISAGREE SLIGHTLY | DISAGREE VERY MUCH | TOTALLY DISAGREE

20 I often think that bad things will happen if I am not careful enough.

TOTALLY AGREE | AGREE VERY MUCH | AGREE SLIGHTLY | NEUTRAL | DISAGREE SLIGHTLY | DISAGREE VERY MUCH | TOTALLY DISAGREE

Scoring instructions

For each item score:

1   for 'Totally agree'
2   for 'Agree very much'
3   for 'Agree slightly'
4   for 'Neutral'
5   for 'Disagree slightly'
6   for 'Disagree very much'
7   for 'Totally disagree'.

The total score on the questionnaire is then calculated by summing the item scores.

NB This means that the score increases as the child shows fewer responsibility attitudes.

Appendix C

Children's Responsibility Interpretation
Questionnaire (CRIQ)

Instructions

We are interested in how you feel about thoughts that have just popped into your mind in the last week. The type of thoughts we're interested in usually interrupt what you are thinking or doing and you can have them more than once. They may be words, pictures, or a sudden feeling that you're going to do something. These are usually called INTRUSIVE thoughts.

We are interested in intrusive thoughts you have that you find hard to deal with. We know that most people have this type of thought at some time, so there's nothing unusual about this. Some examples of unpleasant intrusive thoughts are:

- Repeated pictures in your mind of hurting someone
- Suddenly thinking that your hands are dirty and you may spread germs
- Suddenly thinking that you might not have turned off a water tap, or left an outside door or window open
- Repeated pictures in your mind, that don't make any sense, of someone you love (like your Mum or Dad) getting hurt
- Repeated urge to hurt someone or hit them (even though you would never do this).

These are just a few examples of intrusive thoughts to give you an idea of what we're looking at. People have lots of different thoughts.

Important

Please write down two thoughts like these that you have had in the last week:

1
2

The questions on the next two pages are about any intrusive thoughts like these you have had in the last week. On the next page are some ideas that might go through your mind when you have unpleasant intrusive thoughts.

Frequency

We'd like to know how often you had the ideas below, when you were bothered by these intrusive thoughts. Circle the number that shows how often you had these ideas *over the last week*:

0 I never had this idea.
1 I sometimes had this idea.
2 I had this idea half of the times when I had worrying intrusive thoughts.
3 I usually had the idea.
4 I always had the idea when I had worrying intrusive thoughts.

	Never had this idea	Sometimes had this idea	Half the time	Usually had this idea	Always had this idea
If I don't try to stop these thoughts, I'm not being responsible.	0	1	2	3	4
I could cause something really bad to happen.	0	1	2	3	4
I can't risk this thought coming true.	0	1	2	3	4
If I don't do something now, bad things will happen and it will be my fault.	0	1	2	3	4
I need to be sure something awful won't happen.	0	1	2	3	4
I shouldn't think this type of thing.	0	1	2	3	4
It wouldn't be responsible to ignore these thoughts.	0	1	2	3	4
I'll feel awful unless I do something about this thought.	0	1	2	3	4
Because I've thought of bad things happening, I must do something to stop them.	0	1	2	3	4
Since I've thought of this I must want it to happen.	0	1	2	3	4
Now I've thought of things that could go wrong it is up to me to make sure I don't let them happen.	0	1	2	3	4
Thinking this could make it happen.	0	1	2	3	4
I have to get control of my thoughts.	0	1	2	3	4
It's wrong to ignore these thoughts.	0	1	2	3	4
Because these thoughts come from my own mind, I must want to have them.	0	1	2	3	4

Belief

Over the last week, when these worrying intrusive thoughts bothered you, how much did you believe each of the ideas below was true? Mark the point on the line that shows how much you believed the idea at the time you had the intrusive thought.

I did not believe <u>0 10 20 30 40 50 60 70 80 90 100</u> **I really believed this**
this idea at all   **idea was true**

Statement	0	10	20	30	40	50	60	70	80	90	100
If I don't try to stop these thoughts, I'm not being responsible.	0	10	20	30	40	50	60	70	80	90	100
I could cause something really bad to happen.	0	10	20	30	40	50	60	70	80	90	100
I can't risk this thought coming true.	0	10	20	30	40	50	60	70	80	90	100
If I don't do something now, bad things will happen and it will be my fault.	0	10	20	30	40	50	60	70	80	90	100
I need to be sure something awful won't happen.	0	10	20	30	40	50	60	70	80	90	100
I shouldn't think this type of thing.	0	10	20	30	40	50	60	70	80	90	100
It wouldn't be responsible to ignore these thoughts.	0	10	20	30	40	50	60	70	80	90	100
I'll feel awful unless I do something about this thought.	0	10	20	30	40	50	60	70	80	90	100
Because I've thought of bad things happening, I must do something to stop them.	0	10	20	30	40	50	60	70	80	90	100
Since I've thought of this I must want it to happen.	0	10	20	30	40	50	60	70	80	90	100
Now I've thought of things that could go wrong it is up to me to make sure I don't let them happen.	0	10	20	30	40	50	60	70	80	90	100
Thinking this could make it happen.	0	10	20	30	40	50	60	70	80	90	100
I have to get control of my thoughts.	0	10	20	30	40	50	60	70	80	90	100
It's wrong to ignore these thoughts.	0	10	20	30	40	50	60	70	80	90	100
Because these thoughts come from my own mind, I must want to have them.	0	10	20	30	40	50	60	70	80	90	100

Appendix D

Diaries

Triggering situations What was going on? Who was around?	What was the intrusive thought or image that came into your head?	How distressed did this make you? (0–10 where 0 is 'not at all' and 10 is 'very distressed')	How many times did you get this obsession during the day?
			Monday: Tuesday: Wednesday: Thursday: Friday: Saturday: Sunday:
			Monday: Tuesday: Wednesday: Thursday: Friday: Saturday: Sunday:
			Monday: Tuesday: Wednesday: Thursday: Friday: Saturday: Sunday:

What was going on? Who was around?	What was the intrusive thought or image that came into your head?	What went through your head when you had the thought/picture? What did it mean to you? How much did you believe this at the time (0–100%)?	How did this make you feel? How bad did you feel (0–10%)?	What happened after that? What did you do?

Appendix E

Experiments

BELIEF	DISCUSSION AND EXPERIMENTS	PREDICTIONS
Thinking about harm means it will happen.	Build motivation for experiments by asking the child to make a list of (1) all the times when their thoughts made something bad happen and (2) all the times when they had a bad thought and nothing bad happened. Discussion focuses on the concept of coincidence. If something bad has happened in the past, the idea that this is just bad luck can be proved by repeating the experiment.	If OCD is right about thoughts causing things to happen then: the light will go off, the therapist will be sick, the therapist will fall off of the chair, the shelf will collapse and my mother will be harmed.
	The therapist role models an attempt to make something happen by thinking about it (e.g. turning off a light). The child copies the therapist.	If OCD is a liar then the light will not go off, the therapist will not be sick, the therapist will not fall off the chair, the shelf will be fine and my mother will be fine. All of this means that thoughts don't cause harm.
	The therapist tries to make someone in the room collapse by thinking about it. The child is then asked to make the therapist sick by thinking about it. The therapist jumps on and off a chair while asking the child to make them fall off by thinking or imagining it. The child is ask to cause structural harm by thinking about it (e.g. thinking about a shelf collapsing).	
	While the child's mother goes for walk the child has a bad thought on purpose or waits for a bad thought to naturally occur. Simultaneously, the child does not carry out rituals to prevent harm.	

Intrusive thoughts mean I can read the future.	Ask the child to recall times when they accurately and inaccurately predicted the future. Provide alternative explanations for the occurrence of the event (e.g. bad luck, coincidence, responsibility pie charts). Ask the child to predict the winning lottery numbers this week. Therapist writes down eight numbers from one to 100 and the child attempts to predict every single number.	If OCD is right about my ability to read the future then I will predict the correct lottery numbers and I will predict all eight numbers written down by the therapist. If OCD is a liar my predictions will be wrong.
The more I think about this thought the more likely it will happen.	Ask the child to think about a cake suddenly appearing. Then ask the child to think about this 20 times in row. Discussion focuses on the idea that thoughts do not make things happen and that it doesn't matter how many times you think about it. The therapist and the child practise saying a scary thought out loud 20 times. Discussion focuses on why it is okay to play this kind of game with words (i.e. thoughts are not dangerous, they just feel a bit horrible because they don't fit with who you are).	If OCD is telling the truth then cake will appear or my thought will come true. If OCD is a liar then cake will not appear and my thought will not come true.
Having an urge to do something means I will do it.	Normalise violent and sexual urges by providing lots of examples and carrying out surveys with at least seven people. Ask the child what would happen in the world right now if intrusive violent and sexual urges were truly dangerous (everyone should be dead or in prison).	If OCD is right that urges are dangerous then the therapist will hurt her neck and the child will hurt someone. If OCD is a liar nothing bad will happen because urges on their own do not cause harm.

BELIEF	DISCUSSION AND EXPERIMENTS	PREDICTIONS
	The child is asked to consider all the steps required to carry out a complex action (e.g. move your hand, pick up a knife, move the knife toward your brother, ignore your brother's cries, etc.). Having an urge is not enough. The therapist holds a knife to their own neck and reports a normal urge to press it harder. The child is encouraged to allow violent and/or sexual urges to stay so they can to find out that urges are harmless and alone do not lead to harm (e.g. hold a knife to the therapist's throat, hold their sister near a balcony, touch sister's hand while having intrusive sexual thoughts or feelings.)	
Rituals can stop harm some time in the future.	Ask the child to imagine what they would say to a policeman if a scary man was following them: that is, would they ask the policeman (1) to carry out rituals and then walk away or (2) or to run after the scary man and catch him? Discussion focuses on the idea that if a policeman wouldn't use rituals why would you? Ask the child to prevent the therapist from throwing a pen at their mother by carrying out rituals in the session. If a child believes that future harm could be attributed to their failure to carry out rituals, then the child needs to specify what this harm would be so that exaggerated beliefs about responsibility can be challenged via responsibility pie graphs.	If OCD is right that rituals can stop harm then the pen will not hit my mother. If OCD is a liar then the pen will hit my mother because rituals don't stop harm.

| Germs will make me very ill or kill me. | The child is asked to list all the times when they or their friends were seriously harmed because of germs. Pie graphs are used to challenge excessive responsibility beliefs.

Experiments may include: (1) the therapist touching objects in the office and then touching their face and mouth; (2) encouraging the child to touch several objects in the office and also to touch their face and their parent; (3) encouraging the child to walk around the building pretending that they hate OCD by touching lots of objects and then making a cup of tea to drink; (4) the therapist touching lots of objects in the bathroom including the toilet seat and then wiping their arms and face; (5) encouraging the child to touch the therapist's arm and then eat a biscuit without washing; (6) have the child make an anti-OCD movie by walking around the building, touching lots of germy stuff and eating a sandwich with their germy hands. Encourage the child to design his or her own experiment without telling the therapist. | If OCD is right I will become very ill and I will die. If OCD is a liar I will be very scared because I am worried about dying, but I will be okay. |
|---|---|---|
| Rituals make me feel better. | Ask the child to alternate between carrying out rituals and not carrying out rituals for a period of time in order to see what happens to the size of their worry. For example, if a child believes that holding their head forward will stop their worry about eyeballs rolling into the back of their head, then this child can be encouraged to spend five minutes doing rituals (i.e. holding their head forward) while trying to have a normal conversation. The therapist asks how this | If OCD is right I will feel better when I do my rituals. If OCD is a liar I will feel better when I stop doing my rituals and get on with life. |

BELIEF	DISCUSSION AND EXPERIMENTS	PREDICTIONS
	feels and what they are thinking about while doing this ritual. For the next five minutes the therapist plays a game with the child (e.g. Simon Says) while refraining from rituals. The child is asked what they enjoyed more: doing rituals or not doing rituals. The child can also be encouraged to double their rituals to find out if this makes them feel better or makes them feel worse.	
Reassurance makes me feel better.	Ask the child to alternate between seeking reassurance and carrying on with life normally so that the child can see what happens to the size of their worry. For example, a child could spend five minutes asking their mother lots of questions about harm, followed by five minutes of letting the worry stay in their mind and just carrying on with normal life (e.g. playing a game, having a conversation, or drawing a picture). Discussion focuses on what gave them more worries – asking for reassurance or not asking for reassurance.	If OCD is right I will will feel better if I can ask for lots of reassurance from Mum. If OCD is a liar I will feel better when I don't ask for reassurance and carry on with life normally.
Looking out for signs of danger in my body or in the environment helps me feel better because then I can be prepared.	The child could be asked to focus on their neck for two minutes followed by describing everything that they noticed (e.g. it is hard to swallow, it sounds loud, lots more saliva). Discussion focuses on the idea that looking for body symptoms increases their intensity and increases the chances of noticing normal reactions. The therapist then engages the child in a game for a few minutes and asks the child what happened to the signs in their body that they noticed	If OCD is right then looking for danger in my body will make me feel better. If OCD is a liar then looking danger in my body will make me worse. It is normal to notice strange things when you look for them and it is normal for the feelings to become stronger the more I focus on my body.

	before. Most children report that their bodily symptoms disappeared when they stopped looking for danger. Another experiment involves taking the child for two walks. During the first walk the child is asked to do lots of 'OCD looking' such as looking for harm and scary things. During the second walk the child is asked to act as if they hate OCD and to stop looking for danger and to walk around normally. The child is asked what walk they enjoyed more and why.	If OCD is right then I will go mad with worry (e.g. run around the room like a crazy person). If OCD is a liar then I will feel worried at first, but after a while I will be fine.
I will go mad with worry if I don't wash my hands after touching germy things.	Ask the child to remember how many times they have gone mad or lost their mind before. Ask the child how they will know when they gone mad (e.g. run around in circles or jump out the window). Educate the child about anxiety (refer to Chapter 4). Encourage the child to touch something germy so that they can find out they do not go mad with worry.	

Index